Haitians in Michigan

DISCOVERING THE PEOPLES OF MICHIGAN

Arthur W. Helweg, Russell M. Magnaghi, and Linwood H. Cousins, *Series Editors*

Ethnicity in Michigan: Issues and People
Jack Glazier and Arthur W. Helweg

African Americans in Michigan
Lewis Walker, Benjamin C. Wilson,
and Linwood H. Cousins

Albanians in Michigan
Frances Trix

Amish in Michigan
Gertrude Enders Huntington

Arab Americans in Michigan
Rosina J. Hassoun

Asian Indians in Michigan
Arthur W. Helweg

Belgians in Michigan
Bernard A. Cook

Chaldeans in Michigan
Mary C. Sengstock

Copts in Michigan
Eliot Dickinson

Cornish in Michigan
Russell M. Magnaghi

Dutch in Michigan
Larry ten Harmsel

Finns in Michigan
Gary Kaunonen

French Canadians in Michigan
John P. DuLong

Germans in Michigan
Jeremy W. Kilar

Greeks in Michigan
Stavros K. Frangos

Hungarians in Michigan
Éva V. Huseby-Darvas

Irish in Michigan
Seamus P. Metress and Eileen K. Metress

Italians in Michigan
Russell M. Magnaghi

Jews in Michigan
Judith Levin Cantor

Latinos in Michigan
David A. Badillo

Latvians in Michigan
Silvija D. Meija

Lithuanians in Michigan
Marius K. Grazulis

Mexicans and Mexican Americans in Michigan
Rudolph Valier Alvarado
and Sonya Yvette Alvarado

Norwegians in Michigan
Clifford Davidson

Poles in Michigan
Dennis Badaczewski

Scandinavians in Michigan
Jeffrey W. Hancks

Scots in Michigan
Alan T. Forrester

South Slavs in Michigan
Daniel Cetinich

Yankees in Michigan
Brian C. Wilson

Discovering the Peoples of Michigan is a series of publications examining the state's rich multicultural heritage. The series makes available an interesting, affordable, and varied collection of books that enables students and educated lay readers to explore Michigan's ethnic dynamics. A knowledge of the state's rapidly changing multicultural history has far-reaching implications for human relations, education, public policy, and planning. We believe that Discovering the Peoples of Michigan will enhance understanding of the unique contributions that diverse and often unrecognized communities have made to Michigan's history and culture.

Haitians in Michigan

Michael Largey

Michigan State University Press

East Lansing

♾ The paper used in this publication meets the minimum requirements
of ANSI/NISO Z39.48-1992 (R 1997) (Permanence of Paper).

Michigan State University Press
East Lansing, Michigan 48823-5245

Printed and bound in the United States of America.

16 15 14 13 12 11 10   1 2 3 4 5 6 7 8 9 10

ISBN: 978-0-87013-881-2

LIBRARY OF CONGRESS CATALOGING-IN-PUBLICATION DATA
Largey, Michael D., 1959
Haitians in Michigan / Michael Largey.
p. cm. (Discovering the peoples of Michigan)
Includes bibliographical references and index.
ISBN 978-0-87013-881-2 (pbk. : alk. paper) 1. Haitians—Michigan. 2. Haitian Americans—Michigan. I. Title.
F575.H27L37 2010
977.4'0049697294dc22
2009031983

Cover design by Ariana Grabec-Dingman
Book design by Charlie Sharp, Sharp Des!gns, Lansing, Michigan

Cover photo: Dancers led by Detroit choreographer Penny Godboldo and visiting
Haitian choreographer Frederic Leon in a performance on the Hart Plaza Pyramid
Stage in downtown Detroit, August 2008. Photo courtesy of Karen Dimanche Davis.

Michigan State University Press is a member of the Green Press Initiative and
is committed to developing and encouraging ecologically responsible publishing practices. For more information about the Green Press Initiative and the use
of recycled paper in book publishing, please visit *www.greenpressinitiative.org.*

Visit Michigan State University Press on the World Wide Web at *www.msupress.msu.edu*

ACKNOWLEDGMENTS

Many individuals contributed to this project, and I thank them all for their continued help, patience, and counsel. I thank Marie-José Alcé, Margareth Corkery, Marie Soledad Nelson, Adeline Auguste, Danielle Desroches, Catherine Auguste, the late Roland Wiener, Guérin C. Montilus, Geraud Dimanche, Jean-Claude Dutès, Olga and Dieuseul Benoit, Mathieu Pierre, Dominique Mondé-Matthews, Penny Godboldo, and Serge Bonhomme, as well as several anonymous consultants. I also thank Bill McNeece for most of the photographs. My colleague Mark Sullivan helped prepare the images for the manuscript. Special thanks go to Jean Alcé and Karen Dimanche Davis for reading the manuscript and for their helpful suggestions for improvement. Any mistakes or omissions in this study are entirely my responsibility.

SERIES ACKNOWLEDGMENTS

Discovering the Peoples of Michigan is a series of publications that resulted from the cooperation and effort of many individuals. The people recognized here are not a complete representation, for the list of contributors is too numerous to mention. However, credit must be given to Jeffrey Bonevich, who worked tirelessly with me on contacting people as well as researching and organizing material.

The initial idea for this project came from Mary Erwin, but I must thank Fred Bohm, director emeritus of the Michigan State University Press, for seeing the need for this project, for giving it his strong support, and for making publication possible. Also, the tireless efforts of Keith Widder and Elizabeth Demers, senior editors at Michigan State University Press, were vital in bringing the series to fruition.

Otto Feinstein and Germaine Strobel of the Michigan Ethnic Heritage Studies Center patiently and willingly provided contributor names and gave this project their tireless support. Yvonne Lockwood of the Michigan State University Museum has also suggested and advised contributors.

Many of the maps in the series were prepared by Gregory Anderson at the Geographical Information Systems (GIS) at Western Michigan University under the directorship of David Dickason. Additional maps were contributed by Ellen White.

Other authors and organizations provided comments on various aspects of the work. There are many people that were interviewed by the various authors who will remain anonymous. However, they have enabled the story of their group to be told. The names of many of these contributors are not available, but we are grateful for their cooperation.

Most of all, this work is a tribute to the writers who patiently gave their time to write and share their research findings. Their contributions are noted and appreciated. To them goes most of the gratitude.

ARTHUR W. HELWEG, *Series Co-editor*

Contents

Haiti: Its History and Politics

ocated only two hours south of Miami by jet, Haiti is a country that has had important and long-standing connections with the United States. As the second-oldest republic in the Americas after the United States and the only country ever founded on a successful slave revolt, Haiti has served as a reminder to those who would oppress others that even poor, illiterate slaves could overthrow Napoleon's powerful armies. It has also inspired those who are oppressed through its example of how adversity can be overcome with determination, hard work, and a fearless embrace of freedom. For most contemporary readers, however, the name *Haiti* evokes negative impressions based on its chronic poverty, its political instability, and its long-standing association with Vodou, the religious tradition of Haitian urban and agricultural workers. Although Haiti is the poorest nation in the western hemisphere and its political history has been plagued with numerous coups d'état, its Vodou religious tradition is one of its enduring legacies in the Americas and has served to sustain generations of Haitians as they struggle for political, economic, and cultural independence in a hostile world. In order to understand how Haiti's undeserved reputation as a problematic state has developed, it is necessary to follow Haiti's growth from a former slave colony to an independent black nation.

Haiti occupies the western part of the island of Hispañola in the

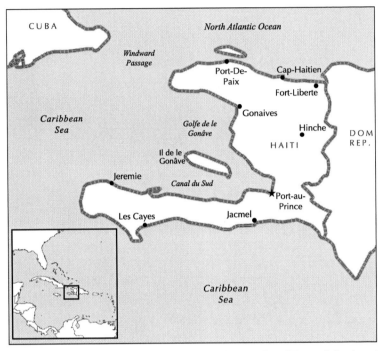

Map of Haiti. Map design by Remote Sensing & GIS Research and Outreach Services at Michigan State University.

Caribbean Sea; it shares the island with the Dominican Republic. Before the arrival of European settlers, the island, then known as Quisqueya in the Arawak language, was inhabited by several different Native American peoples, including the Taïnos, the Caribs, and the Guanahatabeys. Within the first quarter-century of Spanish rule, most of the Native American population was wiped out by a combination of disease and violence. Very little physical evidence remains of the Native American population, but their legacy endures in many of the place names on the island; *Haiti* is an Arawak word meaning "mountainous land."

The Spanish ruled Hispañola from 1492 to 1697, when they ceded the western third of the island to France. Unlike the Spanish, who used Caribbean islands as way stations for their gold- and silver-mining interests in the South American interior, the French developed their new colony, called Saint-Domingue, into a thriving agricultural economy with cash crops such as sugar cane, coffee, and indigo as their principal exports. The success of Saint-Domingue rested, however, on the backs of newly imported slaves from the western and central parts of Africa. Rather than encourage slaves to reproduce and thus replenish the working population, French plantation owners preferred to work their slaves so hard that most of them, especially the field hands who processed sugar cane, lived on average about seven years from when they first arrived in the colony. As a result, when the Haitian Revolution began in 1791, the vast majority of Africans in Saint-Domingue were foreign-born and carried with them the physical memories of their different African cultures.

The brutality of the slaves' lives was matched only by their cultural resiliency. As they were worked to death and physically beaten for any infraction against the laws of the slave owners, Africans maintained many of their cultural practices, especially in the realms of religion, music, dance, agriculture, and aesthetics. Although most Africans arrived in Saint-Domingue with only the tattered clothes on their backs, their minds carried memories of religious rituals, family histories, musical-instrument construction, agricultural and household implements, child-rearing philosophy, and morality.[1] In their new environment, Africans forged a new society based on their previous experiences and their new, hostile living conditions.

One of the important slave responses to the French plantation system was *marronage*. Maroons (in Haitian Kreyòl, *mawon*) were slaves who ran away from the plantations and lived in isolated mountain communities. The geography of Saint-Domingue lent itself to *marronage;* high mountains with few roads allowed slaves to hide from French forces and to organize themselves into self-sufficient societies practicing small-scale farming and hunting. Despite their geographic isolation, maroons were active in the resistance against plantation slavery. A maroon leader named Makandal led a campaign against the French in the 1750s, and Boukman Dutty was one of the important maroon leaders who helped foment the Haitian Revolution against France in the 1790s.

Most French plantation owners tried unsuccessfully to replace enslaved Africans' cultural experience with their own, encouraging slaves to accept Roman Catholicism and to abandon their own religious practices. The resulting blend of Roman Catholic and western and central African religious practices is often called Vodou and is the predominant religious tradition of

Haiti (along with Roman Catholicism) from colonial times to the present.[2] Vodou is a monotheistic religious tradition in which worshipers use music, dance, and spirit possession to connect with ancestral spirits said to live in Ginen (Guinea, or ancestral Africa). Rather than reject their African cosmology and embrace European religious traditions wholesale, slaves chose to merge the practice of Christianity selectively with their own religious traditions in a process known as syncretism. As a result, Catholic saints such as Saint Patrick, the Virgin Mary, and Saint James have counterparts in Vodou religious spirits, or *lwa,* such as Danbala, Ezili, and Ogou, respectively.

This mixing of different religious traditions was frowned upon by the Catholic hierarchy but tolerated to some degree by slaveholders who thought that allowing slaves their own cultural "diversions" would distract them from their difficult living conditions. Such "diversions," however, proved to be a unifying force among enslaved Africans, and in August 1791, during a ceremony at Bwa Kayiman in Saint-Domingue, a slave named Boukman presided over a Vodou ceremony in which the participants pledged to fight against the French and their slave system. From 1791 until 1804, slaves, free persons of color called *afranchi,* and French planters fought against the French army for their own reasons to gain independence for Saint-Domingue. Slaves wished to be free from the yoke of bondage, while *afranchi,* who were offspring of French planters and African slaves, wanted to be free of French meddling in the colony's economic affairs. French planters also wanted to break from the French government's control but not at the price of liberating the enslaved workforce.

After a series of disastrous military campaigns in which French forces were decimated by guerrilla tactics and tropical disease, Haiti declared independence on January 1, 1804. General Jean-Jacques Dessalines, the leader of the Haitian army and the first president of the new Haitian republic, claimed Haiti's legacy as the first modern nation-state founded and led by black people. That legacy was, however, constrained by the economic and cultural isolation that Haiti experienced for most of the nineteenth century.

Economically, Saint-Domingue was the most profitable colony in the French empire. Since the colony's successes were mostly a result of the exploitation of slaves in labor-intensive agriculture, the emergence of a new Haitian republic with its rejection of slavery meant that the former colony's economic wealth could no longer be drawn from bonded laborers. The

French government also levied a 150-million-franc indemnity against the new Haitian state in exchange for French trade. In addition, Haiti went unrecognized diplomatically for much of the nineteenth century; other countries such as the United States and Great Britain traded with Haiti but refused to grant the country diplomatic status. As a result of its isolation, the Haitian economy languished for most of the nineteenth century; rural farmers worked small plots of land at subsistence levels. From the early nineteenth century until the 1920s, when elite Haitians reevaluated their relationships with the rural Haitian workers, Haitian elites and farmers experienced very different social and economic realities. Elite Haitians began a practice of extracting tax revenues from rural farmers in order to support their own lifestyles. The elite, including descendants of the mixed-race *afranchi* and the newly formed dark-skinned black elite (who gained power mostly through their associations with the military), distanced themselves culturally from the rural majority in Haiti while they exploited the lower classes economically.[3]

The cultural division between elite and working-class Haitians is clearly visible in their differing attitudes toward Vodou, the religious practice of the urban and rural majority. Most rural workers participated in Vodou in the nineteenth century. Indeed, since most Catholic priests in Haiti were expelled after the revolution and only those who would work under the supervision of the Haitian state were allowed to remain in the country, most rural Haitians did not have contact with Catholic priests until the Vatican recognized Haiti in 1860. In addition, most Vodou practitioners saw themselves as both Catholic and "servants of the spirits"; Vodou practice assumes a familiarity with and belief in Catholicism as well as in African spirits. Elite Haitians, in contrast, saw the practice of Vodou as an unsavory reminder of their connections to an African past that included slavery and European discrimination. Some elite Haitians eschewed Vodou entirely, while others publicly rejected Vodou practice as they quietly practiced the religion at home.

The nineteenth century was a time of great political turmoil in Haiti. Since it was effectively a pariah state during a time when most other countries in the Americas had slavery-based economies, Haiti had a difficult time participating as an equal trading partner with other nations. Many foreign governments saw Haiti as a place with great potential for economic exploitation; Haiti resisted military intervention from France, Great Britain, and Germany at different times during the nineteenth century. In addition, most of the governments in Haiti at that time were headed by former military insurgents who replaced their political predecessors with insurrectionary coups d'état.

Despite the great political and economic pressures on the Haitian state during the nineteenth century, there were signs of cooperation and collaboration with black people from other nations, particularly the United States. One early example of an African American who saw the potential for black advancement for former U.S. slaves was James Theodore Holly. Originally from Hartford, Connecticut, and trained as a clergyman, Holly traveled to Haiti in the 1850s to examine it as a potential resettlement location for newly freed slaves. With the passage of the Fugitive Slave Law in the United States in 1850, African Americans lived in constant fear of being captured and sold into bondage in the American South. Unlike other former slave-resettlement schemes that centered on repatriation to Africa—mostly to Liberia—the Haitian resettlement plan had the advantage of being close to the United States. In the 1860s, Holly and several thousand of his parishioners from Hartford settled in Haiti and founded what would eventually become the Episcopal Church of Haiti.

The welcome that the Haitian government gave Holly and his followers was in sharp contrast to most Haitian governmental dealings with foreigners interested in settling in the country. Most Haitian leaders were resistant to the idea of granting territorial concessions to foreigners; in fact, since the start of the Haitian republic, foreigners have been constitutionally barred from owning Haitian land. During the latter part of the nineteenth century, however, pressure mounted on the Haitian government to give foreign countries responsibility over Haitian financial institutions. In 1880, the French-controlled Banque Nationale d'Haïti became the principal financial institution of the country, and by 1910, the United States and France jointly administered the Banque Nationale de la République d'Haïti in order to keep German financial interests at bay. Shortly after the outbreak of World War I, the United States seized the assets of the National Bank and invaded Haiti in 1915, ostensibly to quell violence in the aftermath of the overthrow of Haitian president Vilbrun Sam.

The United States occupied Haiti from 1915 until 1934. U.S. officials saw the occupation as a necessary step to protect American trade interests in the region and as a way to keep Germany from gaining an economic and military foothold in the Caribbean. Haitian officials initially welcomed the occupation as a way to regain economic stability in the country. Within the first few years of the occupation, however, Haitian attitudes soured toward the occupation forces as Haitians saw their legislative and judiciary systems overtaken by the United States and their armed forces turned into a national police force. To make matters worse, U.S. officials brought their own views of race to Haiti, discriminating against Haitians who had previously held positions of authority in Haitian society. U.S. officials were unaware of the complex Haitian class system and treated all Haitians, regardless of their social standing, as inferiors.

Although some Haitians hailed the U.S. occupation forces, many were outraged by the interventionist policies of the United States and almost immediately fought back against the occupation. The resistance fighters, known as *kakos* in Haitian Kreyòl, took their names from the *caciques* or warlords of precolonial Haiti. The *kakos* were led by Roger Batraville and Charlemagne Péralte, two middle-class Haitians who helped organize bands of Haitian workers against the occupation. Both men were captured and killed in 1919. Péralte's body was displayed publicly to discourage further outbreaks of violence. A photograph taken of Péralte's body, with his arms outstretched in a position reminiscent of Christ on the cross, helped perpetuate his role as a martyr for the Haitian insurgency against the U.S. occupation.

It was during the U.S. occupation that the elite Haitians began to reevaluate their relationship with the rural Haitian underclass. In 1928, Haitian physician, politician, and educator Dr. Jean Price-Mars published a series of lectures titled *Ainsi parla l'oncle (So Spoke the Uncle),* in which he called upon his fellow elite Haitians to embrace their African ancestry and to reconsider their hostile attitudes toward the practice of Vodou.[4] Until Price-Mars's work was published, most elite Haitians looked upon the Vodou religious tradition as superstition; they also saw the rural Haitians who practiced Vodou as being culturally closer to their African ancestors than the more French-identified elite classes. The U.S. occupation of Haiti provided an opportunity for elite Haitians to identify themselves more closely with the African-derived part of their culture, thereby distancing Haiti from both the United States and France at a time of national crisis. The ensuing indigenist movement in Haiti sparked a wealth of political and artistic production that eventually contributed to the downfall of the U.S. occupation.

Two publications from the 1920s reflect the political and artistic forms of resistance taken by elite Haitians during the U.S. occupation. According to J. Michael Dash, the newspaper *Le Petit Impartial,* which was published between 1927 and 1931, "documents the uncompromising nationalism of the members of the Indigenous movement."[5] *Le Petit Impartial* featured regular attacks on U.S. policies in Haiti and criticized those Haitian institutions that supported the occupation, such as the Catholic church. *La Revue Indigène* was a literary journal that featured less politicized editorials than *Le Petit Impartial* but asserted Haitian culture as a powerful force against the threat of U.S. imperialism. Writers such as Marxist novelist Jacques Roumain and Haitian nationalist Carl Brouard wrote for both publications, bringing their pointed political sensibilities to Haitian elite audiences.

Despite some changing attitudes of elite Haitians toward their African ancestry with the publication of Price-Mars's *Ainsi parla l'oncle,* the Haitian government, in cooperation with the Catholic church, continued its anti-Vodou policies during the early 1940s. Haitian president Elie Lescot, who led the country between 1941 and 1946, mounted an "anti-superstition campaign" against practitioners of Vodou. Lescot's government endorsed using Haitian troops to enter Vodou temples, to destroy ritual objects and musical instruments, and to arrest Vodou *ougan* and *manbo* (male and female Vodou priests, respectively). At the same time that government troops were invading Vodou temples, elite Haitians were forming dance troupes and choirs that featured dances and music from Vodou ceremonies, albeit in a form that did not include religious celebrations. Called *fòklò,* or "folklore," this new form of popular entertainment allowed elite Haitians to participate in local culture without directly interacting with practitioners of Vodou. Lina Fussman Mathon Blanchet, one of the earliest Haitian folkloric choir leaders, brought a group of Haitian folkloric singers to the Pan American conference in Washington, D.C., in 1941, where they performed Haitian songs based on rhythms of the Vodou ceremony.[6] Later, in 1949, the Haitian government constructed the Théâtre de Verdure in 1949 and invited Jean Léon Destiné, one of the most famous exponents of Haitian dance, to lead a national dance company that featured stylized versions of Vodou dance.[7]

It was with the election of President François Duvalier, however, that Haitian politics and cultural representation would be most closely linked. Elected in 1957 in a close presidential race, Duvalier was well known to most Haitians as one of the physicians who had helped eradicate the syphilitic disease called "yaws" in Haiti. Dubbed "Papa Doc" by grateful Haitians, Duvalier was a nationalist who stressed a unique political philosophy called *noirisme* that linked Haitian culture and biology back to Africa. Declaring himself "president for life" in 1964, Duvalier systematically eliminated opposition to his regime by exiling or executing political rivals.

Duvalier also used his interest in Haitian social psychology and culture to underscore several repressive techniques during his fourteen-year rule. He founded the Volontaires de la Sécurité Nationale (Volunteers of National Security, or VSN), also known as the Tonton Makout. Named for a bogeyman figure in Haitian folklore who was believed to capture children in his *makout,* or "straw bag," the Tonton Makout were an unpaid police force that answered directly to Duvalier and acted as a check against the power of the Haitian army. Members of the Tonton Makout dressed in denim and wore straw bags at their waists; their dress was reminiscent of the clothes favored by the Vodou spirit Azaka, a farmer who represents the "common folk" of Haiti. Duvalier drafted poor Haitians into the Tonton Makout and allowed them to extort money from other Haitians in exchange for their loyalty to the president. Since the Tonton Makout were not paid by the government, they were encouraged to exploit their positions as emissaries for the president and to keep local populations in line with the government.

During Duvalier's reign, large numbers of Haitian professionals began leaving Haiti. Fearing for their lives in an increasingly politicized climate in which any activities that were considered critical of the government could be punished by exile or death, many Haitians with the means to leave the country chose to move abroad. Haitians moved not only to predominantly French-speaking areas such as Paris and Montréal but also to New York (especially Brooklyn, Queens, and Manhattan), Boston, and later on, in the 1980s, Miami and Chicago.

After Duvalier's death in 1971, his son Jean-Claude Duvalier succeeded Papa Doc as Haitian president for life. Called "Baby Doc" by his critics, Jean-Claude Duvalier's administration was characterized by political repression and violent crackdowns on political dissent. Baby Doc came to power at the age of nineteen, thanks to a revision to the Haitian constitution hastily drawn up by his ailing father shortly before his death. During Jean-Claude Duvalier's rule, Haitians organized abroad to oppose the dictatorship. This anti-Duvalier, prodemocracy movement was known as *kilti libète* ("freedom culture"), and it drew upon political organizers and artists to promote their message of Haitian liberation from tyranny.

The Haitian political situation during the 1980s eroded steadily with rising crime rates and corruption, as well as increased prices for consumer goods and an expanding drug trade, since Haiti provided a convenient stopover for drugs smuggled from Colombia to the United States. Resistance toward the government grew, and in the mid-1980s, ordinary citizens increasingly took to the streets to protest the government's repressive tactics and violent reprisals against dissent.

Finally, on February 7, 1986, Jean-Claude Duvalier, his family, and a few of his closest political allies left Haiti and flew to France. After nearly thirty years of dictatorial rule, Haitian citizens rejoiced in the streets at the prospect of being rid of their despised ruling family. The resentment against the Duvalier regime was very strong, especially among those who had suffered personal losses at the hands of the dictatorship. In the months following Duvalier's departure, a process known as the *dechoukaj* or "uprooting" of the dictatorship was under way. Drawing its name from the Kreyòl verb *dechouke,* a word used by Haitian farmers to refer to pulling out a plant by its roots so that it cannot grow back, the *dechoukaj* of the Duvalier regime included persecution of the Tonton Makout militia. Members of the Tonton Makout were beaten and sometimes killed by angry mobs exacting revenge for the crimes of the dictatorship against Haitian citizens. As a result, many members of the Tonton Makout sought refuge in the ranks of the Haitian army, a traditional opponent of the regime that was seen by most Haitians at that time as representing the interests of the common people.

Between the departure of Duvalier in 1986 and the elections of 1991, Haiti was led by a series of temporary governments that drew most of their leaders from the ranks of the Haitian army. Elections in November 1987 were canceled after armed gangs attacked voters in polling sites around Port-au-Prince. The following February, Haitian general Henri Namphy oversaw an election in which longtime politician Leslie Manigat was elected president with an estimated 5-percent voter turnout. Manigat's rule lasted only until June 1988, when he was ousted by Namphy in a coup d'état. Namphy's short-lived administration was followed by that of Prospère Avril, another Haitian general who relied on the support of his troops to maintain his grip on power. Finally, in March 1990, Haitian Supreme Court justice Ertha Pascal Trouillot was sworn in as Haiti's first female president, and the country prepared for elections the following spring. During this tumultuous period, the Haitian constitution was revised to make way for democratic elections.

On October 15, 1990, a former Roman Catholic priest named Jean-Bertrand Aristide announced his candidacy for the Haitian presidency. Aristide was well known as an advocate for the poor and as a critic of Haitian and U.S.-owned businesses that exploited Haitian labor. He was expelled from the Salisian order by the Catholic church, which considered his brand of liberation theology too volatile for the Haitian clergy. Aristide was a target of an assassination attempt on September 11, 1988, when armed thugs attacked the St. Jean Bosco Church in which Aristide was holding mass. Several parishioners were killed, and the church was burned. Aristide's escape from the massacre was hailed by his supporters as evidence of his destiny to help the Haitian poor.

In February 1991, Aristide was elected president of Haiti with 67 percent of the popular vote in an election that was, by all accounts, free and fair. Aristide's election signaled the beginning of a political era in Haiti in which the needs of both rich and poor Haitians would be a matter of national concern. Aristide's tenure as president, however, would be cut short by a coup d'état in September 1991.

From 1991 until 1994, a series of leaders were put in place with the approval of General Raoul Cédras, the chief of the Haitian army, and his followers. This military junta persecuted supporters of Aristide and murdered many Haitians who supported the return of the elected president. The United States called for an embargo of Haiti that effectively targeted the poor members of society; wealthy Haitians were able to circumvent the blockade through contraband shipments by air, sea, and overland via the Dominican Republic. Aristide's departure in 1991 was followed by an increase in Haitian refugees to the Bahamas, Turks and Caicos, and the United States. Members of Aristide's Lavalas ("Cleansing Flood") party were targeted by the military junta, and many fled the country and resettled in the United States.

In 1994, after several failed attempts to negotiate with the reigning military junta, U.S. forces invaded and began the second U.S. occupation of Haiti of the twentieth century. President Aristide was permitted to return to Haiti but was allowed to serve out only the remainder of his five-year term, which ended in 1996. René Préval, a former Haitian prime minister during Aristide's first term, was elected to the presidency in 1996.

In 2001, Aristide ran for the Haitian presidency a second time and won. His second term was characterized by increasing violence, often at the hands of armed gangs, which took their name from a mythological fire-breathing demon or chimera. *Chimè yo* were based in the poorer neighborhoods of Port-au-Prince, especially Cite Solèy, where large numbers of desperately poor Haitians live. Aristide was criticized for not bringing the *chimè yo* under control, thus turning many formerly pro-Aristide supporters against his government. In October 2004, armed gangs hostile to Aristide marched on Port-au-Prince and drove the president into exile again. He was flown out of Haiti in a plane provided by the U.S. government. Aristide and many of his supporters claimed that he had been kidnapped by the United States. In 2006, René Préval was elected president for a second time and has worked to quell gang violence and restore order in the country.

Haiti's turbulent political history has been exacerbated by its relationship with the United States. Although many of the problems Haiti has faced have been brought on by poor governance and an elite class that exploits the vulnerable poor population, the United States has added to Haiti's problems by treating the second-oldest republic in the western hemisphere as an economic and political inferior. As we turn our attention to the situation of Haitians abroad, specifically those in large metropolitan areas in the United States, the tenuous relationship between Haiti and the United States continues to affect Haitians in their daily lives.

Haitians in the United States

Haitians have been coming to the United States since before the founding of the U.S. republic. In fact, it was a Saint-Dominguan trader and explorer named Jean Baptiste Pointe DuSable (1745–1818) who founded what would become the city of Chicago. DuSable was born in St. Marc on the island of Hispañola to a free African mother and a French father. DuSable was educated in France and spoke several languages fluently, including French, Spanish, and English. He arrived in New Orleans in the 1770s and traveled up the Mississippi River until he reached present-day Peoria, Illinois, where he farmed about thirty acres of land. He established a trading post at the mouth of the Chicago River. He married a Native American woman from the Potawatomie tribe and had two children from this marriage. DuSable eventually moved from Chicago, was imprisoned by the British during the Revolutionary War for siding with the Americans, and died in Missouri after selling his properties in Illinois to Jean Lalime, a French Canadian fur trader.

Saint-Dominguans also participated in the American Revolution, contributing 750 soldiers to the American side in the Battle of Savannah in 1779. Henri Christophe, who would eventually become the third Haitian head of state, fought in the Battle of Savannah himself.

The Haitian Revolution, which lasted from 1791 until 1804, prompted a vast exodus of people from colonial Haiti or Saint-Domingue, mostly in the form of wealthy landowners and their slaves. Exiled Saint-Dominguans settled in several cities in the United States. In Charleston, South Carolina, several exiles worked in theatrical and musical professions.[8] Musicologist Oscar Sonneck reported that a concert in Charleston on December 17, 1793, featured two musicians who were well known on the prerevolutionary stages of Port-au-Prince.[9] In Philadelphia in 1797–98, one of the best-known refugees from Saint-Domingue, Médéric Louis-Elie Moreau de Saint-Méry, published a multivolume description of Saint-Domingue titled *Description topographique, physique, civile, politique et historique de la partie française de l'isle Saint-Domingue* ("Topographic, Physical, Civil, Political and Historical Description of the French Part of the Island of Saint-Domingue"). Moreau de Saint-Méry's work continues to be one of the main sources for information about precolonial Haiti.

Saint-Dominguans fled in the largest numbers to New Orleans, home of one of the largest enclaves of French speakers in the Americas at the time. Seen by many Saint-Dominguans as a northern Caribbean city, New Orleans became part of the United States in 1803 after France sold the Louisiana Purchase to the U.S. government. New Orleans's long-standing reputation as a center for French culture in North America made it an attractive destination for French slaveholders, since they were allowed to keep their slaves after they immigrated.

In the first decade of the nineteenth century, New Orleans went through a period of rapid growth. Part of this population growth was a result of the large numbers of refugees fleeing the Haitian Revolution, especially those who were part of the French planter class in Saint-Domingue. The population of New Orleans grew from 8,000 in 1800 to 12,000 in 1806. By 1810, the city had grown to 24,552.[10] With this rapid growth in population, especially among those Saint-Dominguan refugees who brought with them a taste and talent for the dramatic arts, came an increase in the number of musical activities in the city. Before the Haitian Revolution, Saint-Domingue was the center of theatrical entertainment in the Americas. Between 1764 and 1791, there were more than 3,000 dramatic and musical performances in Saint-Domingue.[11] Opera, dance, and pantomime troupes regularly visited Saint-Domingue from France, and local performers developed their own enthusiastic followings among the planter classes in the colony.

New Orleans quickly developed its own thriving theater culture after the influx of the Saint-Dominguan refugees. Although some historians of New Orleans dismiss the influence of the Saint-Dominguan immigrants,[12] there is ample evidence that Saint-Dominguan artists made their mark on the dramatic arts in the United States through their participation in New Orleans theaters.[13] In addition, Saint-Dominguans brought popular dances and rhythms from colonial Haiti to the United States, including the *bamboula*, the *kalinda*, and the *juba*. During the rest of the nineteenth century, Haitian immigration to the United States was small and sporadic.

It was with the installation of François Duvalier in 1957 that the large-scale immigration of Haitians to the United States began in earnest. As discussed earlier, Duvalier's rule over Haiti was characterized by violent repression of resistance, including kidnapping, imprisonment, torture, and execution for opponents of the regime. As Duvalier tightened his grip on power in the early 1960s, it became clear to many Haitians that the price of staying in Haiti would be to accommodate Duvalier's brutal tactics and, eventually, to participate in the repression directly. Many Haitian intellectuals decided to leave Haiti rather than help Duvalier consolidate his control of the country. Between 1961 and 1970, 34,499 Haitians resettled in the United States.[14] The resultant "brain drain" of elite and middle-class Haitians led Haitians to establish diaspora outposts in such places as New York, Boston, Montréal, Paris and Zaire.

The mass exodus of upper- and middle-class Haitians to places such as the United States prompted a form of political organization that had been impossible within Haiti itself. François Duvalier managed to stay in power and avoid antagonizing the U.S. government by maintaining a strict anti-communist stance; Duvalier positioned himself as a counterweight to Fidel Castro's communist regime in nearby Cuba. The U.S. government rewarded Duvalier for his anticommunism with relatively little political interference. As a result, communist organizing in Haiti was dealt with harshly; many left-wing organizers left the country as their comrades were swept up in government roundups of political adversaries.

In the United States, some politically left-leaning Haitians organized cultural groups that stressed Haitian rural culture as a rallying point for Haitians in the diaspora. Calling their work *kilti libète* ("freedom culture"), many politically minded Haitians became involved in criticizing the Duvalier regime by participating in Haitian-themed activities that called into question the ruling regime's legitimacy. Ethnomusicologist Gage Averill has described the work of many of these early freedom-culture music groups, the most famous of which were Atis Endepandan ("Independent Artists"), Solèy Leve ("Rising Sun"), and Tanbou Libète ("Drum of Freedom").[15] The music of the freedom-culture groups drew on music of the Vodou ceremony, the Haitian cooperative-labor teams known as *konbit,* the migrant-labor music tradition known as *mizik twoubadou* or troubadour music, and music of the Lenten processional tradition known as Rara.[16] Each of these Haitian musical traditions evoked strong associations in the minds of Haitian listeners abroad. Rara and *konbit* are uniquely Haitian practices and are often associated with rural culture in Haiti. By connecting themselves with activities from the Haitian countryside, freedom-culture activists self-consciously positioned themselves as authentic cultural actors whose political positions paralleled those of the downtrodden Haitian masses. Thus, upper- and middle-class Haitians in the United States rhetorically aligned themselves with the disempowered Haitian working classes and set themselves in opposition to those in power whose policies contributed to the suffering of the Haitian people.

After the departure of Jean-Claude Duvalier from Haiti in 1986, the expatriate Haitian political movement became more involved in electoral politics in Haiti. By the time Haitian president Jean-Bertrand Aristide was elected in 1990, the diaspora was recognized by Haitians at home and abroad as a significant contributor to the Haitian economy and political life. Aristide labeled the Haitian diaspora the "tenth department" as a way to acknowledge the importance of overseas Haitians in the affairs of the Haitian state. Haiti has nine *départments,* or states; overseas Haitians are thus metaphorically included in the Haitian state as the tenth department. Aristide's interest in overseas Haitians was more than rhetorical, however. He established a Ministry of Haitians Living Abroad that officialized the connections between Haitians at home and abroad. According to Nina Glick Schiller and Georges Fouron, "In maintaining this ministry, the Haitian government is declaring that emigrants, whatever their legal citizenship, remain Haitian."[17]

One of the ways that Haitians in the United States maintain their connections with Haitians in Haiti is through remittances. Most Haitians living abroad send money to family and friends living back home in order to help pay medical bills, send children to school, pay for rent, or maintain small businesses conducted in the home. Since banks in Haiti have not been disposed to cater to nonelite Haitian customers, many money-transfer companies have sprung up over the last thirty years to meet the demand of the Haitian remittance market. Companies such as Boby Express, C.A.M., and Socatransfer all maintain offices in the United States and in Haiti so that individuals can wire money directly to relatives in Haiti. These companies operate mostly in Haitian enclaves such as those in New York City, Miami, Boston, and Chicago. Other money-transfer companies such as Western Union are popular among Haitians living outside the large metropolitan areas in the United States that support large Haitian populations.

AIDS, Boat People, and Black Magic: Misconceptions about Haitians in the United States

Like other immigrant groups to the United States, Haitians face challenges as they make the transition from being immigrants to legal residents. Language barriers, racial discrimination, and American ignorance about Haitian customs can leave many Haitian immigrants discouraged and anxious about their decision to move to the United States. Unlike other immigrant groups, however, Haitians have the added burden of dealing with misconceptions about them that have far-reaching consequences for their well-being in the United States.

One of the principal misconceptions about Haitians that has created a problem for their smooth transition into U.S. society is their putative association with the virus that causes acquired immune deficiency syndrome, or AIDS.[18] A number of early cases of AIDS among Haitians who were heterosexual and were not intravenous drug users led some researchers to suspect that Haitians were at a high risk for contracting and spreading the disease. As physician and medical anthropologist Paul Farmer has pointed out, scientists and media reporters fueled a belief that Haitians were carriers of HIV (the virus that causes AIDS) and that it was Haitians who transmitted the disease to the United States.[19] Even respected medical journals published articles that were based on speculation linking HIV transmission to Vodou ceremonial rituals. As Farmer pointed out:

> In the October 1983 edition of *Annals of Internal Medicine,* for example, physicians affiliated with the Massachusetts Institute of Technology related

the details of a brief visit to Haiti and wrote "It seems reasonable to consider voodoo practices a cause of the syndrome."[20]

Unfortunately, these initial responses to the AIDS crisis became enshrined in medical practice in the United States. By the mid-1980s, most health agencies associated AIDS transmission with four distinct populations: homosexual males, intravenous drug users, hemophiliacs, and Haitians. By 1990, Haitians and people who had lived in Haiti were barred by the U.S. Food and Drug Administration from donating blood to U.S. blood banks.[21]

Since the late 1980s, legitimate medical research has debunked the idea that all Haitians are likely carriers of the disease and has indicated instead that Haiti was an unfortunate victim of an international sex-tourism industry that brought AIDS to Haiti through prostitution. As the poorest country in the western hemisphere, Haiti has long been a destination for tourists in search of inexpensive sex from impoverished men and women who sell their services for a fraction of what they would cost in the United States. Male prostitutes, many of whom identified themselves as heterosexual, contracted the disease and then transmitted the virus to their female partners. The stigma against homosexuality in Haiti made it difficult for men who prostituted themselves to advocate on their own behalf, and as a result, many died from opportunistic diseases associated with AIDS. In the early 1980s, Haiti lacked the public-health infrastructure to educate the population about having unprotected sex. Since then, awareness of safe-sex practices has helped bring down the rate of HIV infection in Haiti, but AIDS continues to be a public-health concern, just as it is in the United States.

The recognition of AIDS as a global health crisis came at about the same time that political turmoil in Haiti prompted many poor Haitians to leave Haiti. During the mid-1980s, as the Jean-Claude Duvalier dictatorship was losing its control over the country, the government engaged in political crackdowns that were aimed at shoring up Duvalier's regime. While upper- and middle-class Haitians could leave the country legally by airplane, poorer Haitians took the only means of transportation available to them: boats, called *kantè,* named for the Canter, a popular brand of Mitsubishi truck that was used for Haitian public buses called *tap-tap.* Like the *tap-tap,* the *kantè* was said to hold a large number of people and to travel quickly to its destination, in this case to the shores of the Turks and Caicos Islands, the Bahamas, and southern Florida. At the time, many poor Haitians joked that there were two classes of Haitian people: *Boeing pipèl* ("Boeing people," those able to afford the price of a plane ticket) and *bòt pipèl* ("boat people," or those destined to risk their lives in unsafe boats on the open sea).

In the 1980s, media coverage of Haitian boat people landing on the shore tended to depict them as fleeing crushing poverty rather than seeking refuge from a hostile political climate in their home country. The U.S. government ignored political abuses in Haiti for years in exchange for assurances that Haiti would remain an anticommunist state. The longevity of both the François Duvalier and the Jean-Claude Duvalier governments was a result, in part, of their adherence to a policy toward Cuba that reflected U.S. interests. Both Duvalier dictatorships were rewarded for their hard-line stances against Cuba's Fidel Castro with foreign aid from the United States. When Cuban refugees from what came to be called the Mariel boatlift arrived in the United States in the 1980s, they were welcomed as political dissidents against the Castro regime. According to Alex Stepick, Haitian refugees were depicted as "people who appeared strikingly poor and who were described as fleeing the Western Hemisphere's poorest and least educated country."[22] Haitians in the United States chafe at the policy of treating Cubans who enter the country illegally as political refugees while Haitians are most often considered to be fleeing economic hardship.

Religion

Haitian immigrants brought a multitude of religious practices with them. Most Haitians are Roman Catholic and make up a large enough group to warrant masses conducted in Haitian Kreyòl.[23] Although non-Catholic Christians make up a minority of Haitian immigrants, they belong to a variety of denominations, including Episcopal, Methodist, Baptist, Seventh-Day Adventists, and Pentacostal, as well as dozens of other nondenominational congregations. Church not only gives spiritual succor for Haitians but can also provide important social and cultural networks for people who desire a visceral connection to home. Many congregations feature Haitian Kreyòl services and often include Haitian food as part of their fellowship offerings.

In addition to the wide variety of Christian religious practice, many people practice Vodou, a syncretic religion that combines aspects of Roman

Catholicism and various western and central African religious traditions. Spirits, or *lwa,* act as intermediaries between people and God, or *Bondyè,* through religious services featuring music, dance, feasting, and spirit possession.

Haitians in the United States have to deal with the commonly held misperception that the traditional religious practices of the Haitian rural workers are synonymous with depictions of "voodoo" as a malevolent spiritual practice. This concept of "voodoo" was founded shortly after Haiti's independence in 1804, when U.S. slaveholders, fearful of a similar insurrection among their own slave populations, encouraged depictions of Haitians as barbarous savages who practiced "black magic," used "voodoo dolls," and turned unsuspecting people into "zombies." Elsewhere, I have argued that such depictions of Haitian religion serve to manufacture a "simulacrum" or a model of reality that has its own behaviors, perceptions, and rules.[24] Simulacra are, in effect, "more real" than reality, since they are more readily available to people through the mass media. In the case of Haiti, Vodou religious practices are consistently misrepresented as evil in most movies and television programs. Without any evidence to the contrary, most American audiences are unable to distinguish between this manufactured concept of Haitian culture and the actual practice of traditional religion in Haiti.

As early as 1937, anthropologist Melville Herskovits noted this tendency for foreigners to associate Haiti with "voodoo":

> More than any other single term, the word "voodoo" is called to mind whenever mention is made of Haiti. Conceived as a grim system of African practices, it has come to be identified with fantastic and cruel rites and to serve as a symbol of daring excursions into the esoteric. Not only has emphasis been placed on its frenzied rites and the cannibalism supposed on occasion to accompany them, but its dark mysteries of magic and "zombies" have been so stressed that it has become customary to think of Haitians as living in a universe of psychological terror.[25]

Herskovits and his wife, Frances, spent three months in southern Haiti in the 1930s researching the practices of the rural population. What they found was a complex system of religious rituals that had strong connections to African religious practices, especially in their emphasis on the veneration of ancestors and service to the spirits who act as intermediaries between Haitians and God. Unfortunately, this vision of Vodou religion has had to compete with the more pervasive and pejorative view of Haitians in the form of "voodoo."

As a religion that has been consistently maligned by non-Haitians—and repudiated by many upper-class Haitians as well—Vodou has had to adapt itself in order to escape persecution by hostile forces. One such adaptation that Vodou has undergone in its movement from Haiti to the United States is how Vodou ceremonies are held. In rural Haiti, ceremonies are most often held in *lakou,* or village compounds, in which closely related families worship together in open-air *peristil,* or dancing areas; spirits who are said to reside in Africa travel to the ceremony in order to inhabit the bodies of worshipers.

In the United States, Vodou ceremonies are usually conducted in the basements of residences that are owned or occupied by Haitians. In one such ceremony I attended in 1991, about sixty worshipers crammed into an apartment building's basement in the Bedford-Stuyvesant neighborhood of Brooklyn. Musicians playing animal-skin-headed drums, shakers, and struck pieces of metal sat in one corner of the room, while participants competed for the dozen or so folding chairs available at the other end of the basement. The *manbo,* or female Vodou priest, directed individuals to complete their ritual tasks; the ceremony was a *manje yanm,* an annual harvest festival, in which yams, bananas, and dried fish were offered to Vodou spirits in thanks for a bountiful harvest. As the drummers provided rhythms that signaled specific spirits to join the ceremony, the *manbo* was possessed by several spirits in succession, each with its own particular personality traits and clothing preferences. When the *manbo* was possessed by Ogou, a military spirit associated with iron and warfare, she wore a red sash and drank spiced rum directly from the bottle, spraying it over the crowd in an aggressive gesture of spiritual protection. After all of the spirits had been saluted by the congregation, the feast of yams was distributed to the participants. Although this ceremony featured a complete Vodou drum battery, many U.S. Vodou ceremonies have only vocal music and hand clapping in order to keep non-Haitian neighbors from complaining to the police about noise violations.[26]

Despite the relatively high number of participants in Vodou ceremonies in the United States, many middle-class Haitians feel a persistent ambivalence toward the religious practice.[27] Since one requirement of Vodou practice is to be baptized as a Roman Catholic, many non-Vodou-practicing Catholics bristle at the idea of being associated with what many consider a lower-class activity. For many Protestants, Vodou is seen as little better than devil worship; when a person becomes *konvèti* ("converted") to a Protestant denomination, he or she is called upon to renounce any association with Vodou. For other Haitians, Vodou is seen less as a threat to their Christianity and more as a cultural resource that distinguishes them from other ethnic minorities.

One of the most active cultural groups promoting Vodou as a Haitian cultural resource is New York's La Troupe Makandal. Named for an early Haitian revolutionary who was also a Vodou priest, La Troupe Makandal is led by artistic director and master drummer Frisner Augustin. Augustin was born in Haiti and emigrated to the United States in 1972. He assumed the artistic directorship of La Troupe Makandal in 1981 and with executive director Lois Wilcken, an ethnomusicologist who specializes in Haitian music and culture, runs the organization with a commitment to educating the public about the richness of Haitian culture.[28] One of the group's popular programs commemorates a meeting of Haitian slaves in 1791 who came together at Bwa Kayiman (Bois Caïman) to plot the overthrow of the slave society of Saint-Domingue. La Troupe Makandal's celebration of this historic ceremony takes place every August in Brooklyn's Prospect Park, a popular location for many Haitian celebrations.

In an effort to promote Haitian culture to diaspora Haitians as well as to foreigners, La Troupe Makandal sponsors regular drumming lessons at Hunter College and leads a children's musical workshop called Krik! Krak! (named for the traditional Haitian invocation for a communal storytelling session). Augustin also regularly works with the Haitian children's dance group Tonèl Lakay. In recognition of his musical artistry and his commitment to promoting Haitian culture in the United States, Augustin received a National Heritage Award from the National Endowment for the Arts in 1999.[29]

Media

Media such as newspaper, radio, television, and magazines serve to connect diaspora Haitians not only to events in Haiti but also to one another within the United States. Newspapers such as *Haïti Progrès,*[30] *Haitian Times,*[31]

Haïti-Observateur,[32] *Haïti en Marche,*[33] and the *Boston Haitian Reporter*[34] have large circulations in most Haitian population centers in the United States. As Haitian anthropologist Michel Laguerre has observed:

> The ideas promulgated by these newspapers are developed on American soil and they project models of democracy for Haiti based on or influenced by American ideas and ideals. Through their influence on the Haitian political system, these newspapers have imbued the local scene with American-bred political ideas.[35]

During the 1970s and '80s, *Haiti-Observateur* (founded in 1971) and *Haiti Progrès* (founded in 1983) were explicitly anti-Duvalier in their editorials and reporting. Laguerre notes that *Haiti-Observateur*'s "information—and sometimes consciously fabricated disinformation—created much confusion among officials of the Duvalier government."[36]

There are also several Haitian radio stations, including Radio Tropicale, Radio Soleil d'Haiti ("Sun Radio of Haiti"), Radio Pa Nou ("Our Radio" or "Radio for Us"),[37] Radio Carnivale, and Radio Keenam.[38] Radio Soleil is a subcarrier station; until it opened its Web site, the only way to hear the station was to purchase an adapted radio receiver. Radio Soleil's programming is about 50 percent in Haitian Kreyòl, 40 percent in French (to appeal to French-speaking elite Haitians and also to Martiniquans, Guadeloupeans, and other French-speaking immigrants to the United States), and 10 percent in English.[39] Founded in 1989, Radio Tropicale was the first French- and Kreyòl-speaking radio station to broadcast in the United States. With the establishment of Port-au-Prince-based Radio Tropicale d'Haiti in 1993, the Radio Tropicale franchise was able to broadcast news coverage directly from Haiti. Other radio stations have opened in recent years, but because of the pressures of earning enough advertising revenue, many stations last only a short time on the air.[40]

Radio is perhaps the most important medium of entertainment and communication for Haitians at home and abroad; most Haitians in Haiti get their news from radio. In addition, radio serves an important social function by circulating personal messages over the airwaves to places that may not have telephones or reliable mail service. For many Haitians in rural areas, radio announcers inform them of deaths, community meetings, and visitors from overseas looking to meet family members. Most of the radio stations in Haiti have dedicated times for public announcements so that individuals can pass along personal information over the air. For example, Radio Nationale, the official government radio station, and Radio Lumière, an evangelical Christian station, both have airtime devoted to reading announcements and messages sent in from listeners trying to reach friends and loved ones in different parts of the country.[41]

Cultural Pride and Studies

For some Haitians, pride in their Haitian identity is tempered with pressures to assimilate into the larger African American population. Among school-age Haitian children, the desire to conform to American, specifically African American, culture can result in a phenomenon that Alex Stepick has called going "undercover." Stepick claims that many young Haitians are under intense pressure to turn away from their Haitian roots because of "their perception of intense prejudice against Haitians specifically in their schools and more generally in South Florida."[42] Stepick points out that young Haitians may adopt African American clothing styles and ways of speaking in order to fit in with their African American classmates.

For other Haitian youth, however, there is a tendency to demonstrate pride in their Haitian heritage; Maria Fernández-Kelly and Richard Schauffler call these Haitians "strivers" for their determination to succeed in school and to promote Haitian culture openly.[43] In addition, many young Haitians go through phases of going "undercover" only to assert their Haitian pride at a later time.

The Haitian Studies Association (HSA) is headquartered at the University of Massachusetts in Boston; it is the principal academic institution devoted to the scholarly study of Haitiana. The HSA holds an annual conference that brings together scholars from a variety of disciplines who are interested in different aspects of Haitian culture, politics, economics, and a host of other perspectives. The first few HSA conferences were held at Tufts University in Medford, Massachusetts, but subsequent conferences have been organized in Detroit, Milwaukee, and Atlanta, as well as locations in Haiti, including Port-au-Prince and Montrouis.[44]

The Africana Studies program at the University of Massachusetts in

Boston not only supports the HSA, but it also sponsors a language course in which non-Haitians can undertake intensive study of Haitian Kreyòl, the country's principal language. Held every summer since 1988, the Haitian Language and Culture Summer Institution offers students the opportunity to study with native speakers of Haitian Kreyòl; out-of-town students are placed with Haitian families in the Boston area to facilitate their language learning.[45] The Summer Creole Institute is jointly administered by the university's Haitian Studies Program and the Haitian Studies Association.

Besides asserting their cultural pride in their everyday lives and in their studies, members of Haitian communities throughout the United States demonstrate their connections to the family and friends they left behind in Haiti through major relief efforts, as well as individual acts of support for communities they help sustain.

Mother Theresa Maxis Duchemin:
A Haitian American Nun in Michigan

Although Haitians have never been as numerous in Michigan as Arabs or Germans, they have played an important, if overlooked, role in the development of vital institutions in the state. One of the most important individuals in early Michigan history was Mother Theresa Maxis Duchemin (1810–1892), a Haitian American who helped found the Congregation of the Sisters, Servants of the Immaculate Heart of Mary (IHM), in Monroe in the mid-nineteenth century.

As a child of a biracial Saint-Dominguan (now Haitian) mother and a white British father, Marie Almaide Maxis Duchemin was raised by her mother in Baltimore.[46] According to Marita-Constance Supan, "the Duchemins had fled the 1793 slave uprisings in St. Domingo and had brought with them to the port of Baltimore a ten-year-old girl of color, Marie Annette ('Betsy') Maxis, whose parents had perished in the carnage. The Duchemins raised her, benefited from her work in the home and provided for her training as a nurse. In spring 1810, Betsy bore a daughter, Marie Almaide Maxis Duchemin, by a visiting cousin of the Baltimore Howards."[47]

Unlike most young girls of color at that time, the young Marie Maxis Duchemin had the opportunity to attend school and became fluent in both English and French; she also studied mathematics and was exposed to religious education.[48] In 1829, at the age of nineteen, Maxis Duchemin took **27** her religious vows and entered the novitiate with the name Theresa; she also joined with several other Catholics to found the Oblate Sisters of Providence, a Catholic religious order devoted to the education of "young girls of colour."[49] At that time, Maryland law forbade the education of children of color with whites, so religious institutions were the only options for young people, especially girls, to receive an academic and spiritual education.

Supan writes that "on the surface, the Oblates' work appeared typical for New World congregations, focusing on preserving immigrants' religious-cultural heritage while integrating them into the evolving American mainstream. However, for French-speaking free women of color and their students, racial prejudice defined the task."[50] Mother Theresa and her colleagues developed a unique educational opportunity for their young students, an environment of spiritual and intellectual stimulation tempered with an awareness of racial prejudice. She was elected general superior for the Oblates in 1841.[51]

Earlier in the 1830s, however, the Oblate Sisters of Providence ran into difficulties, as one of their founders, Father Joubert, fell ill and the Catholic hierarchy in Baltimore withdrew its support for the sisters. In 1843, as the Oblate sisterhood was on the verge of collapse, Mother Theresa met two Belgians who would dramatically affect her life: Bishop Peter Paul Lefevere and Father Louis Florent Gillet. Lefevere was the bishop of Detroit, a Catholic outpost in Michigan that was badly in need of priests and nuns to carry out spiritual work. Gillet was newly arrived in the United States with a desire to help expand Catholic outreach on the American frontier. Both men recognized Mother Theresa's strengths as a charismatic leader and as a potential organizer for a new religious order. Mother Theresa's three-year term as mother superior ended in June 1844, but an election for her successor did not take place until December of that year.[52] She was replaced as mother superior by Sister Louise; Mother Theresa was elected to be Mother Louise's assistant.[53]

Mother Theresa's transition to life on the Michigan frontier included, however, a distancing from her biracial heritage and a denial of her Saint-Dominguan past. Her decision to "pass" as white was not unusual for light-skinned women of color at that time, especially women who were in a position to exercise influence in community affairs. The new environment of southeastern Michigan unfortunately did not include a new attitude toward race and color; Mother Theresa's downplaying of her background allowed her opportunities to affect missionary and educational activities in her new home.

On September 9, 1845, Mother Theresa left the Oblate sisterhood for her new life in Michigan. Detroit was the largest trading post in an area that included not only the upper and lower peninsulas of Michigan but also parts of Wisconsin and Minnesota.[54] It had been under the supervision of Bishop Frederic Rees, a German-speaking prelate who had allowed the diocese to deteriorate rapidly. By the time Mother Theresa and Father Gillet arrived in Michigan, most of the charity work and educational projects under Bishop Rees's supervision had been abandoned, and the debts owed by the Catholic church had mounted dramatically.[55]

During the early days of Mother Theresa's tenure in Michigan, she had an enthusiastic and willing collaborator in Louis Gillet. He brought an expansive spiritual agenda, including an interest in founding French Temperance Societies throughout the region and missionary outreach into what was often described as the "wilderness" that was southeastern Michigan at that time. Unfortunately, Gillet's penchant for taking bold initiatives was viewed critically by the Catholic hierarchy, and he was forced out of Michigan in 1847.[56] During their first two years in Michigan, however, Gillet and Mother Theresa brought Anne Shaaff, one of Theresa's fellow sisters from Baltimore, to join her in Michigan to found a new religious order.[57] Eventually, the sisters took their vows in December 1845 and established the Sisters, Servants of the Immaculate Heart of Mary (IHM).

Initially, the IHM sisters enjoyed a limited autonomy; Bishop Lefevere often communicated with them by letter rather than in person, and the congregation expanded its outreach mission to other communities. However, the Redemptorist priests who had initially supported the IHM congregation and who, with Father Gillet, shared Mother Theresa's vision of a widening missionary and educational effort, told Bishop Lefevere of their intention to withdraw from Michigan.[58]

It was with the appointment of Reverend Edward Joos that the conflict between the independent-minded Mother Theresa and the Catholic hierarchy would come to a head. Joos, like most Catholic prelates of his day, believed that a nun should submit to a priest's judgment in all matters material and spiritual. One of his first acts as director of the IHM congregation was to change the mission of the group from education to establishing orphanages.[59] With Joos's appointment as cleric in charge of the IHM congregation, Mother Theresa came into conflict with the Catholic hierarchy almost immediately.

The incident that prompted Mother Theresa's split from the IHM congregation came four years after Father Joos's installation. In 1859, she responded to a request from Reverend J. V. O'Reilly, a Redemptorist priest in Susquehanna, Pennsylvania, who asked that she and several of her sisters establish a new congregation among Irish railroad workers there. In July 1958, Mother Theresa and Sister Aloysius Walter traveled to Pennsylvania to help with the new congregation. When she appealed to Bishop Lefevere and Father Joos for permission to make a similar trip to help found another Pennsylvania congregation, she was refused.[60]

According to Supan, Mother Theresa's reaction to her superiors' refusal of her request reflected her unique perspective as a dynamic and forceful leader who was constrained by her position as a nun.

In a blatant departure from the nineteenth-century script for a woman— particularly a "good," religious woman—she stood her ground with the director in a clash of wills, perspectives, and purposes that proved disastrous. "I did not," she related later, "give up and still persisted in demanding justice" until it became clear to her that her judgment about community affairs would be held hostage to Lefevere's and Joos's determinations.[61]

Lefevere immediately removed Mother Theresa from her official duties and sent her and those sisters perceived to be loyal to her to the newly formed congregation in Pennsylvania. The bishop forbade the remaining sisters to communicate with Mother Theresa, effectively banishing her from the congregation she had helped found fourteen years earlier.

After 1859, Mother Theresa Maxis Duchemin never lived again in Michigan. She lived for some time in Pennsylvania and then moved to Canada to live with a community of Grey Nuns in Ottawa. She hoped to reestablish contact with the Monroe congregation but was repeatedly denied permission to contact her former colleagues. From 1868 to 1885, Mother Theresa lived in Ottawa; she was eventually allowed to return to Pennsylvania, where she spent the last seven years of her life in West Chester.[62]

Despite her short time in Michigan, Mother Theresa Maxis Duchemin accomplished a great deal, especially for the spiritual and academic education of Michigan's youth. Her perseverance and dedication to the education of young women in Michigan are represented today by the existence of Marygrove College, an independent Catholic liberal arts college in the city of Detroit.[63]

Haitian Communities in Michigan: Issues and Challenges

Haitians often use proverbial expressions to make commentaries on situations in which they find themselves. In some cases, Haitian proverbs parallel those in English. For example, *"Men anpil, chay pa lou"* ("With many hands, the load is not heavy") roughly translates to the English "Many hands make light work." Other proverbs have a more specific cultural resonance with Haitians, such as *"Pyebwa tonbe, kabrit manje fèy li"* ("When the tree falls, the goat eats its leaves"), a phrase used to describe a situation when someone in authority who has abused his or her power is brought down to the level of the common people. In this case, even a majestic towering tree becomes fodder for animals if it cannot stand on its own.

Another proverb that comes to mind when discussing the relative size and strength of the Haitian population of Michigan is *"Pi piti, pi rèd"* ("The smaller something is, the tougher or stronger it is"). Usually used in reference to a person of small stature whose personal energy and charisma give others the impression of a large, imposing individual, this proverb aptly describes the social and cultural strength of the relatively small population of Haitians in Michigan in comparison with the larger Haitian populations of New York, Miami, Boston, and Chicago. According to the 2000 Census, there are about 2,000 Haitians living in Michigan, most of whom are concentrated in three areas: Detroit, Lansing, and Grand Rapids. According to historian

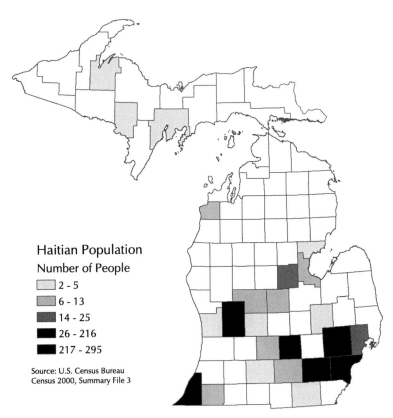

Haitian population of Michigan. Map design by Remote Sensing & GIS Research and Outreach Services, Michigan State University.

Chantalle Verna, however, there are probably closer to 4,000 Haitians living in Michigan, if one counts all of the Haitians and Haitian Americans who identify themselves as Haitian.[64]

In a study of Haitians in Detroit, Lansing, and Grand Rapids, Verna described Haitians who came to the Great Lakes State as falling roughly into one of three categories: those who were invited, those who were seeking, and those who were sent. Haitians who were invited included "individuals offered educational and/or employment opportunities." People who were seeking included those who "sought out or recognized the potential for opportunities, mostly in the 1970s and '80s." Finally, those who were sent included "individuals who were directed toward their place of refuge" (i.e., refugees from the political turmoil in Haiti itself, most of whom came after the 1991 coup d'état).[65] Detroit is the oldest of the Haitian communities in Michigan and has the largest number of active cultural organizations in the state. While all three of the largest Haitian communities in Michigan include people from every social stratum, Detroit's Haitian population has a larger percentage of upper- and middle-class Haitians than does Lansing or Grand Rapids. According to Verna's model, Detroit's Haitian population has the largest concentration of people who were invited and those who were seeking. Detroit's initial appeal to Haitian immigrants came from the auto industry. After World War II, Detroit's reputation as a source of high-paying, stable employment drew thousands of immigrants from all over the world. In the 1980s, auto workers could earn between fifteen and twenty dollars an hour in the assembly plants.[66] Although most Haitians I spoke to came to Michigan after the 1980s, there were a few who moved to Detroit after the consolidation of the Duvalier dictatorship in the early 1960s. Of those early immigrants, most were professionals and were able to establish careers in their chosen fields of engineering, medicine, law, and business.

Haitians settled in different parts of Detroit, including the far northeast area of the city, suburbs to the far north (Northville, Farmington Hills), the more central northwest areas, as well as around downtown, Hamtramck, and the neighborhood near Wayne State University. Others live in northwestern Detroit in an area bounded by Telegraph Road, the Southfield Freeway, Five Mile Road, and Eight Mile Road.[67] The Catholic churches that most Haitians attend in Detroit are St. Gerard in northwest Detroit and Sacred Heart in downtown Detroit. St. Gerard recently merged with the Immaculate Heart of Mary Church and is now known as Corpus Christi Church. While the church does not hold services in Haitian Kreyòl, it does sponsor activities to support the Haitian community. For example, in February 2008, St. Gerard hosted beginning Haitian Kreyòl language lessons for congregation members who were planning to attend a medical mission in Haiti that May. Sacred Heart has an active interest in Haitian welfare; the Sacred Heart Church Haiti Program has supported construction projects and sponsored emergency relief for victims of hurricanes Gustav, Hanna, and Ike in the hardest-hit part of Haiti just outside Gonaïves.[68]

Many of the Haitians I have interviewed mentioned that they had connections with the Haitian communities of New York, either having family in one of the metropolitan boroughs or having lived there themselves for some time. For many Haitians still in Haiti, New York represents the entire United States; it is not uncommon to have Haitians in Haiti ask a foreign visitor *"Kote nan Nuyòk w sòti?"* ("Where in New York are you from?"), meaning "Where are you from in the United States?" For some Haitians in Detroit, however, New York is a nostalgic place where Haitians live in large numbers and Kreyòl speakers are in great supply; for some Haitians who left New York City to move to Detroit, New York—rather than Haiti—is where they call home. Adeline Auguste, a Detroit Haitian who was born in Haiti but lived for many years in New York City before moving to Michigan, told me that when she initially arrived in Detroit, she returned often to New York to purchase food supplies for Haitian cuisine, items such as *kabrit* ("goat") and *djon-djon,* a black mushroom used in a popular Haitian rice dish.[69]

Lansing is home to a small but vibrant Haitian community that consists mostly of Haitians who arrived in the United States during the economic embargo of Haiti in the mid-1990s. In 1991, a military junta under the command of General Raoul Cédras ousted President Jean-Bertrand Aristide and began a systematic suppression of dissent. Opponents of the military junta were jailed, killed, or driven into exile; many chose to come to the United States for political asylum. Others chose to leave Haiti because of the extreme climate of political violence and the threat of retaliation from those loyal to the military government.

As Haitian immigration to the United States increased during the junta, social-services organizations in cities such as New York and Miami were overwhelmed. In order to redistribute the refugees fairly and to ensure that they received the services they needed, many Haitians were redirected to places such as Lansing and Grand Rapids, where Haitian populations were small but where Haitian Kreyòl-speaking social workers could help them adjust to their new lives. Although Lansing no longer has a Kreyòl-speaking social worker, there was one full-time Haitian social worker, Alix Mondé, in Lansing during the 1990s, along with some volunteers from the local community.

In 1994, I had the opportunity to witness firsthand the process of Haitian resettlement when I saw an announcement in the *Lansing State Journal* asking for help with recently arrived refugees. Lutheran Social Services and Catholic Refugee Services, the principal agencies in charge of Haitian resettlement at that time, put me in contact with two recent arrivals. Jean and Robert (not their real names) described a story that is common among Haitian refugees to Michigan during this period. Although they came from different parts of Haiti—Jean was from northern Haiti, while Robert was from the south—both men had left on small boats from their respective towns and had been picked up by the U.S. Coast Guard as they made their way through the Windward Passage between Haiti and Florida. They were taken to the U.S. military base at Guantanamo Bay, where they met; they were held for several weeks before being sent to Florida. From there, they were sent to Lansing, where a Haitian social worker placed them with an American host family who could help them adjust to their new surroundings.

For both young men, newly arrived in the United States and without any understanding of English, adjusting to life in Lansing was a challenge. Neither had ever driven a car, had a bank account, or lived in an urban area; despite social services' best efforts to mediate culture shock, both men often asked me to explain American customs and habits that seemed baffling to them. Jean called me one evening, his exasperated tone indicating that he was very upset with his host family. When I arrived at the house, Jean explained that his host was insisting that he limit his daily bathing rituals to one shower a day. In tropical Haiti, many people bathe several times a day, especially after working outdoors or making a trip via public transportation. To Jean, the thought of bathing only once a day during the hot summer months seemed inconceivable and somewhat disgusting. Jean's host, who was concerned about how much hot water such frequent baths consumed, thought that Jean was being profligate with his water use. Fortunately, a crisis was averted once Jean and his host understood each other's point of view, but such cultural conflicts were a frequent subject of discussion during Jean's and Robert's first few years in the United States.

Haitian refugees in Lansing in the 1990s found work mostly in the service sector. For many immigrants, employment opportunities were limited because of their lack of English-language skills. Many worked at large local businesses, such as the Michigan-based hypermarket chain Meijer; language fluency was not crucial for jobs in the shipping and warehouse departments. Others worked at places such as Peckham, an organization that provides "vocational training, assessment and rehabilitation for persons with barriers to employment in Mid-Michigan"; in this case, Haitians' "barrier to employment" was most often their difficulties with spoken English.[70] In Grand Rapids, as in Lansing, Haitian refugees arrived in large numbers after the ouster of Aristide in 1991. Several individuals in Grand Rapids fall into Verna's category of those who were sent to Michigan for political reasons. In addition, a large number of unaccompanied minors came to Grand Rapids and were placed in foster care through Bethany Christian Services.[71] By 1999, there were about 500 Haitians living in Grand Rapids, according to one social-services provider.[72] Since their arrival in Grand Rapids in the 1990s, many of those who were sent have moved to other parts of the country, especially to southern Florida and New York. For those Haitian refugees who decided to stay in Michigan, some have sought postsecondary education at Grand Rapids Community College[73] and Kent Career Technical Center,[74] working full-time while going to school. For Dieuseul and Olga Benoit, Grand Rapids provided both husband and wife an opportunity to work. Although at first they were only able to secure factory jobs that paid minimum wage, they were able to purchase a house and two cars through scrupulous saving and a tight household budget. Dieuseul Benoit explained:

> God destroys something to make something new. The coup d'état in Haiti pushed me to do something new. I left Haiti as a political refugee, so I had some choice about where to settle in the United States. When the translators for immigration found out where we wanted to move, they asked me, "Why are you going to Michigan? There aren't any Haitians!" I responded that it was peaceful and that there were opportunities for my children to excel.[75]

Challenges in a New Life

Many Haitians have embraced their new country with similar zeal, yet others have faced significant challenges in trying to adapt to their new lives in Michigan.

The process of being uprooted from Haiti under violent circumstances created a degree of trauma that made adjustment to their new environment difficult for many. Jean-Claude Dutès, a Haitian psychologist at Michigan State University, has studied the effects of "acculturative stress," or the discomfort a person feels when confronted with a new and unfamiliar cultural system. Dutès notes, "The process of changing one's ways of being is inevitably stressful if and when the demands placed on oneself exceed internal and external resources."[76] In his capacity as a clinical therapist, Dutès has worked with many Haitian immigrants to the Lansing area. He noted that for many recent immigrants, the culture shock they experienced upon arriving in Michigan was intense. Dutès told me that while a few Haitians experienced some psychological issues regarding their rough sea journeys, most were traumatized by being separated from their loved ones back in Haiti. Several of the patients he spoke to had little time to put their affairs in order before they took to the seas; often, families did not know that one of their members had left on a boat. Many of the Haitians who were resettled in Lansing also had difficulty with their new surroundings. For a Haitian from a rural background, who was used to using trees and other natural objects as guideposts, moving to Lansing, with its paved streets, flashing lights, and steady traffic, was overwhelming. In addition, many were wary of the Lansing police, given their previous experiences with corrupt Haitian police officials.[77]

Dutès discovered, at least for some of the Haitian men he spoke with, several factors that led to their improved mental health. First, contact with people back in Haiti gave many immigrants a sense of connection and purpose; their stress levels were improved once they could establish regular exchanges with family in Haiti. I found this to be the case when I established contact with my aforementioned friend Robert's family in Haiti in 1996. I spent that summer in Port-au-Prince and managed to contact Robert's brother in rural southern Haiti using a ham radio. When I asked about Robert, the brother replied in a flat tone, *"Li mouri"* ("He died"). When I told Robert's brother that he had not died and that he was living and working in Michigan, he was skeptical at first, but when I told him of Robert's unique medical history, he quickly realized that I did indeed know his brother. After this initial contact, Robert was able to establish contact with the rest of his family, first by sending cassette tapes to his mother and eventually by calling her on a cell phone that he bought for her.[78]

Second, finding a job and sending money to family members in Haiti in the form of remittances helped many Haitians in Lansing feel more settled and less stressed. Finding a job and establishing contact with family in Haiti allowed many refugees to feel that they were making an active contribution to their families' welfare. As Nina Glick-Schiller and Georges Fouron have noted in their study of diaspora Haitians in the United States, there is an expected pattern of obligation between Haitians who have traveled abroad to find work and those who remain behind in Haiti.[79] Most Haitians in Lansing are expected to contribute toward the maintenance of the family home, sending money for home improvements and for establishing in-home businesses such as informal retail sales of soap, toothpaste, sugar, soft drinks, and prepared foods.

Third, socializing with other Haitians helped many younger Haitians feel less isolated and disconnected from their surroundings. For several years during the mid-1990s, Haitian men met weekly on the school grounds of Fairview Elementary School in Lansing for an informal soccer game. Such games gave young Haitian men the opportunity to meet with their peers, work off some excess energy, and gather news about the political situation in Haiti. For many, playing soccer on Saturday afternoon was the highlight of their week.

Finally, establishing an informal system of *parenaj* and *marenaj,* or sponsorship, for recent Haitian arrivals helped to mitigate feelings of isolation and abandonment and promoted social and cultural connections with other Haitians. Several Haitians who were established in the area served as unofficial sponsors for refugees. The terms *parenaj* and *marenaj* refer to the male and female godparent relationships, respectively; this relationship is important in Haiti, since it is the godparents who usually take responsibility for a child if that child's parents die, and godparents also provide monetary support for their godchildren's graduations, marriages, and other costly events.[80] In the Lansing context, established Haitian residents take some degree of responsibility for ensuring that recently arrived Haitians get the services they need. In some cases, sponsors invited recent arrivals to their homes for meals of Haitian food accompanied by Haitian popular-music recordings. Verna noted that one of the sponsors she spoke to helped others to find suitable housing, transportation, job applications, and medical care.[81]

For other Haitians who came to Michigan not as refugees but by choice, Michigan provided a calm contrast to the situations they left behind. While those who moved from New York to Michigan regretted leaving friends and extended family members behind, they also said that the pressures of living in New York, with its snarling traffic and hectic pace, made it difficult to have a full and satisfying social life. One individual who came to Detroit from New York told me that her husband had had a five-mile, two-hour commute each way from his job at a hospital; he rarely had the opportunity to speak with his children before leaving for work or after he arrived home at night. One evening, he called home to pass the time as he waited to leave work until the traffic subsided; his young son asked him, "When am I going to see you?"[82] Another Haitian compared her experiences in New York and Detroit, saying that in Detroit, *"Tout bagay alez, tout moun gen kay yo"* ("Everything is relaxed, everyone has their own houses"), adding that in New York, people with a heavy mortgage might have to supplement their incomes by taking in boarders.[83] For many Haitians who moved to Detroit, the city provided an attractive and affordable place to raise their families.

Haitians in Detroit not only maintained their contacts with family and friends in New York City, but they also have forged connections with Haitians in the diaspora. Marie-José Alcé described an elaborate network of social organizations designed to put people in the Haitian diaspora in touch with other individuals from the same parts of Haiti. She belonged to two diaspora organizations in the United States: one from the northwestern part of Haiti, where she grew up, and one from the Port-au-Prince neighborhood, where she spent her early adulthood.[84] Both organizations hold yearly reunions in different parts of the United States, often in either New York or Miami.

Haitian Culture in the Great Lakes State

For most Haitians living in the United States, one of the most pressing concerns after finding a suitable job and housing is to determine how to maintain a daily connection with Haitian culture. Those who have immigrated to Michigan from Haiti as adults have a different connection to Haitian language and culture than those who were born in the United States to Haitian parents. While Haitian immigrants themselves may have a hard time fitting into U.S. cultural situations, their children generally do not. Individuals born to Haitian parents who moved to the United States at a young age or those who were born in the United States to Haitian parents usually have a fluent command of English, partly because of their education in U.S. public schools. It then becomes difficult for those Haitian children to connect to their Haitian identity when they may have very little physical connection to Haiti itself.

Several U.S.-born Haitians I interviewed mentioned that they often felt as though they were caught between an American and a Haitian cultural orientation. U.S.-born Haitian Danielle Desroches said, "Growing up in Detroit, I felt like a misfit because Haitian parents raised their kids on the 'nerdy' side. The way we dressed, our lack of American slang, and our primary focus on our families made us different from our classmates."[85] Desroches also mentioned that she often gravitated toward other "international" students in school, since they tended to understand what it meant not to "fit in" with the rest of their classmates. She said that when she was young, she thought of herself as an "American kid"; once she was a teenager, it became more important to participate in Haitian cultural activities, especially music and dance. Those Haitians who were able to maintain their fluency in Haitian Kreyòl were able to participate in Haitian cultural events with older Kreyòl- and French-speaking members of the community. They were also more likely to participate in community events such as parties, family gatherings, and dances.

For some U.S.-born Haitians in Michigan, the challenges of maintaining a connection to Haitian culture are different from the challenges for those who live in large Haitian American enclaves such as New York or Miami. For some Haitians in Michigan, there is a sense of urgency to maintain and protect Haitian culture from being forgotten by the younger generation. Desroches said that it was easier for Haitians in New York to connect to Haitian culture because they are surrounded by it: "They don't make choices about Haitianness; I have to make a choice. . . . If my New York cousin marries a non-Haitian, it would be easier for their children to be exposed to the culture. In Michigan, marrying a non-Haitian would make things difficult. Haitianness would be dying."[86]

The concept of "Haitianness" or "Haitianity" is something that Haitian anthropologist and Wayne State University professor Guérin Montilus observes is part of the everyday life of most Haitians in Michigan, despite their assimilation into other aspects of life in the United States. Montilus claims that *ayisyenite,* or Haitianity, is best observed in Haitians' home life.[87] In my conversation with him, Montilus mentioned the Haitian rural custom of burying a deceased family member on the family's ancestral lands. Often,

Haitian-born immigrants to the United States express a desire to be returned to Haiti after they die for burial on their family's land. This connection to land and place of origin gives Haitians abroad a visceral connection back to the place of their forebears. Montilus explained that the commonly understood Haitian Kreyòl phrase *"M se pitit tè a"* ("I'm a child of the land") reflects this sensibility that a person's identity is rooted in what land his or her ancestors claim. For Haitians who made the voyage from Haiti to the United States, the idea of returning to Haiti for their eternal rest taps into a collective memory that sustains Haitians as they find their way in a foreign environment.[88]

Perhaps the most salient feature of Haitian cultural identity among Haitians living abroad is language. I have described the linguistic situation in Haiti this way:

> The majority of the Haitian population speak Haitian Creole or Kreyòl, a language that grew out of the contact between French planter society and the enslaved African population of Saint-Domingue. In the nearly two centuries since Haitian independence, French retained its associations with wealth, power, and prestige; official transactions were conducted exclusively in French during the nineteenth and twentieth centuries. In 1959, sociolinguist Charles A. Ferguson identified the linguistic situation in Haiti as "diglossic," where a high-prestige language (French) was used for administrative and educational purposes and a low-prestige language (Kreyòl) was relegated to informal discourse. Today, most linguists refer to Haiti as having two separate linguistic communities: a small, bilingual elite who speak French and Kreyòl and the majority of the population who speak only Kreyòl.[89]

With its adoption as a Haitian "national" language in 1979, Kreyòl was given an official orthography or writing system. Until the 1970s, those wishing to write Haitian Kreyòl were forced to choose between several different orthographic systems, including the McConnell-Laubach orthography (invented by Northern Irish Methodist missionary Ormande McConnell and revised by American Frank Laubach) and the more French-looking orthographic system of Charles Fernand Pressoir, who criticized the McConnell-Laubach orthography as being "too Anglo-Saxon looking."[90] Today, Haiti has two official languages: French, which had been the sole official language since

1804, and Haitian Kreyòl, which was established as the "national" language of Haiti in 1979 when the Institut Pédagogique National d'Haïti standardized the orthography for Kreyòl.

Haitian immigrants generally speak Haitian Kreyòl; some speak Kreyòl and French, especially if they come from either a middle- or upper-class background in Haiti. Immigrants often face problems when confronted with learning a new language; this is especially true for adult learners of English. Their U.S.-born children, on the other hand, grow up speaking English fluently; their experiences in U.S. schools give them an advantage over their Kreyòl- (or French-) speaking parents, especially in situations that demand an extensive knowledge of English. Several children of Haitian immigrants mentioned in interviews that they have had to accompany their parents for important meetings with non-Haitian officials. In some cases, the parents' English was strong enough to complete the transaction, but older nonnative speakers of English may have had to rely on their children for moral support in such situations.[91]

Like many other children of immigrants in the United States, some U.S.-born Haitians do not speak the language of their culture, Haitian Kreyòl, fluently. On one hand, in an effort to assimilate quickly into American culture, some Haitian immigrants insist that their children speak English exclusively. For many parents, ensuring that their children are not stigmatized for not speaking English fluently is a more pressing concern than making sure that they maintain their Kreyòl language. On the other hand, since many second-generation Haitians do not have a direct experience of life in Haiti, many Haitian families stress the importance of keeping up their language skills in Haitian Kreyòl. One person told me that Haitian immigrants are vye rat ("old rats," or very skilled) in their understanding of Haitian culture; they want to pass along their cultural knowledge to their children using their native language.[92] I met equal numbers of Haitians in Michigan who spoke Haitian Kreyòl at home and those who did not (but most who don't speak have a strong passive understanding of spoken Kreyòl).

Haitians also engage in physical, visible demonstrations of their cultural heritage. One of the most important ways that Haitians maintain their cultural connections with one another is through preparing and consuming Haitian food. When asked to name the most significant cultural practice among Haitians in Michigan, Haitian physician Marie Soledad Nelson replied:

Food! We love food; we love to eat. When you go visit someone, you have to eat; it's almost like an insult not to eat. When I go to New York, I have to make sure I eat very little [beforehand], because when I visit my relatives, the first thing they ask me is "What are you eating?" They cook in large portions because they know that other people are coming.[93]

When asked how often she eats food cooked in a Haitian style, she added:

I make Haitian food about 70 percent of the time. I like *griot, pate.* Every time I go home [to New York], I try to make something like my mother. There are a few things I have to learn. . . . I don't know how to make *lanbi.* I can make *diri ak pwa* and fish.[94]

Griot (pronounced "gree-oh") is a pork dish that is marinated, cooked in herbs, and then fried. *Pate* (pronounced "pah-tay") are small pastries filled with spiced ground meat; Jamaicans have a similar pastry called patties, but they are spiced differently from Haitian *pate. Lanbi* (pronounced "lahm-bee") refers to the meat inside the conch shell. It is difficult to prepare since it must be tenderized properly; otherwise, it is tough and rubbery. *Diri ak pwa* refers to a staple of the Haitian diet: rice and beans. While there are many types of rice-and-beans dishes in Haiti, *diri ak pwa* (or *diri ak pwa kole,* "rice and beans stuck together") usually features rice seasoned with pork fat, onions, garlic, and cloves. It is served several times a week in most Haitian households; the mere mention of *diri ak pwa* to most Haitians can work up an appetite.

Other popular Haitian foods include *bannann peze,* or crushed plantain. The plantain is a starchier, less sweet cousin of the Cavendish banana found in most U.S. grocery stores. It is cut into thick, diagonal slices, seasoned with salt and lime water, and fried in oil until it becomes tender on the inside; then it is crushed and refried. Haitians also consume several varieties of *vyann,* or meat, including beef, pork, chicken, and goat.

Several people told me that large chain stores carry most of the staples for Haitian cooking, such as rice, beans, and plantains. Specialty stores, especially markets frequented by African, Mexican, Arab, and Filipino clients, tend to have some of the more difficult-to-find grocery items such as *vyann kabrit* ("goat meat") and *aransò* ("smoked herring"). One Haitian I interviewed said that she regularly made *kibbee,* a Lebanese dish made from ground bulgur wheat and ground beef. *Kibbee* is popular in Haiti, albeit in a slightly different form. Lebanese food is common in Haiti because of a large influx of Lebanese immigrants to the county in the late nineteenth century. As Susan Kalčik observed in her work on foodways among ethnic communities in the United States, subsequent generations of immigrants may have very different relationships to their home-culture cuisine.[95] For some second-generation Haitians in the United States, diets may consist of only a few select Haitian dishes, but methods of preparation may remain squarely Haitian. Danielle Desroches, a Detroit Haitian who was born in the United States, said that she doesn't usually cook Haitian food, but whenever she prepares any type of meat, she washes it with limes in order to kill germs and tenderize the food, just as her mother does.[96]

Food is not only a culturally significant resource to entertain friends and relatives; it is also an important vehicle for the promotion of health. Several people told me that they regularly used Haitian folk medicine to cure common ailments. For example, one individual, whose mother was a *doktè fèy* ("leaf doctor") in Haiti, often used leaves from common plants for therapeutic teas. Tea made from ginger or thyme leaves is good for digestion, as is tea made from garlic. A tea made from the leaves of the soursop or *kowosòl* plant is good for a cold, as is a remedy with orange rind and honey.

Another important way that Haitians in Michigan display their cultural solidarity is through the celebration of holidays. The two most important Haitian holidays cited by people I spoke to were Haitian Independence Day (January 1) and Haitian Flag Day (May 18). Independence Day commemorates the anniversary of Haiti's victory over France in the war for independence from 1791 to 1804. Since Haiti was the only country ever founded on a successful slave revolt, Haitian independence symbolizes not only the freedom of the Haitian people but also the beginning of the end of the system of slavery that held black people in bondage throughout the world. Independence Day parties often feature *soup joumou* ("squash soup"), a traditional meal that contains pureed squash, turnips, cubes of meat, noodles, and potatoes in a savory stew. In Lansing, a group of Haitians from the Eglise Méthodiste Libre du Calvaire braved a winter storm to hold a late-evening church service on December 31, 2007, that was followed by a dinner featuring *soup joumou* at midnight.

Haitian Flag Day party announcement, Haitian Network Group of Detroit, May 2008.

Among Haitians in the diaspora, Flag Day provides an important opportunity for people to demonstrate publicly their pride in Haitian culture. The Haitian flag has undergone several changes of design since its first use on May 18, 1803, in the town of Arcahaie.[97] According to most accounts, General Jean-Jacques Dessalines, who led the country to independence in 1804, formed the first Haitian flag by taking the French tricolor and ripping out the white center section, thus symbolically tearing the French government out of Haitian affairs. In Haitian Kreyòl, the word *blan* translates literally as "white," but it is also used to connote "foreign." Eventually, Dessalines (and, later, François Duvalier) substituted black for the blue of the original flag, but in 1986, the Haitian flag returned to its pre-Duvalier form: horizontal fields of blue on top and red on the bottom, with the coat of arms of Haiti in the center. The Haitian motto, *"L'Union Fait la Force"* ("Through Unity Comes Strength") appears below the coat of arms.

Flag Day celebrations today are held among Haitian diaspora communities throughout the United States, including Tampa, Miami, New York, various parts of New Jersey, and Boston. The Haitian community of Detroit celebrated Flag Day on May 31, 2008, with a party held by a local Haitian family.

Flags are also prominently displayed for public events such as concerts, parties, and picnics. Catherine Auguste of Detroit reflected that when Wyclef Jean of the hip-hop group the Fugees took the stage to accept a Grammy Award in 1996 wrapped in a Haitian flag, it may have inspired other young Haitians to embrace the flag as a symbol of their Haitian pride.[98] Certainly, Haitian pride was in evidence in 2000 at the 62nd Annual National Folk Festival in East Lansing, Michigan, when the popular Haitian *mizik rasin* ("roots music") group Boukman Eksperyans took the stage. A group of about forty Haitians stood directly in front of the band with an enormous Haitian flag; they sang along with the music, much to the surprise of the band members, who were unaware of a Haitian presence in Michigan. Haitians have also taken to displaying small flags on their cars, either affixed to the top of the vehicle in the current style of many sports teams' flags or with a small flag hanging from the rearview mirror or draped in the center of the back seat.

Flags are also used in pan-Caribbean celebrations as a way to boost cultural pride and to represent the presence of Haitians at the event. During the 18th Annual Caribbean Family Reunion picnic at Belle Isle Park in Detroit on June 28, 2008, many Caribbean flags were on display from such places as Jamaica, Trinidad, the Dominican Republic, Barbados, and Panama. Haitians flew a flag from the top of one of the picnic shelters to signal to other Haitian participants where they could find *pate*, rice and beans, and other Haitian dishes.

Pan-Caribbean celebrations tend to emphasize the similarities between people from different Caribbean countries, yet such celebrations also provide specific opportunities to appreciate diverse strengths. For most of the Haitians I interviewed for this book, their pride in being Haitian was an important part of their own personal identity. Knowing about their ancestral culture was a large part of maintaining a sense of self in a diverse, multiethnic society like the United States. For Marie-José Alcé, a Haitian mother of two U.S.-born children, giving her offspring a sense of what it means to be Haitian was important to keep them on the right path in life. She said:

> You don't know where you are going if you don't know who you are. You have to know who are; then you can go from there. Many children are messed up because they don't know. I am trying to teach my kids who they are; you are a product of us. You are American, but you still have some Haitian in you.[99]

Most Haitians are aware of the negative stereotypes that others hold about their country, so for some, demonstrating their Haitian pride publicly gives them a sense of satisfaction. Margareth Pierre Corkery, a Haitian social worker at Wayne State University who works as an AIDS counselor, put it bluntly:

> I'm 100 percent Haitian; everything in my cubicle [at work] is from Haiti, Haitian calendar, flag, etc. I don't care how people say how ugly [Haiti] is, just because you don't know it. If you know it, you know it is a gorgeous country, and the people are nice. I just love my country. I'm so proud to be Haitian, and I will continue to be until my death.[100]

For others, Haitian pride is something that comes in the form of nostalgia for the Haiti they left behind years before. Marie-José Alcé expressed her feelings about returning to Haiti after a long absence:

> When I go to Haiti, I cannot explain to you how it feels. When the plane is about to reach Haiti, even in the plane the feeling is different. When I'm getting out of the plane, it is something I cannot explain.[101]

For some African Americans, especially in the Detroit area, connecting with Haitian culture is an important way to emphasize the commonalities of the black experience in the Americas. Penny Godboldo, an associate professor of dance at Marygrove College in Detroit, is a certified instructor of the Dunham Dance Technique, which is named for Katherine Dunham, an African American anthropologist and dancer who studied Haitian dance for many years. According to Godboldo, Dunham's interest in Haiti helped to break down many misconceptions that non-Haitians had about Haiti, especially its Vodou heritage. Dunham used dance to express connections between the African-derived spirituality of African Americans and Haitians. Godboldo, who is not Haitian herself, nevertheless feels connected to Haitian culture through her experiences with Dunham's work in Haiti; for Godboldo, Dunham helped non-Haitians see how "music and movement work together to raise the human spirit." Godboldo expressed her feelings of solidarity with Haitians this way:

My goal is to help people recognize that Haitian culture is part of a continuum of the African diaspora and that we have a lot more in common than is different. . . . I feel that by furthering the knowledge and respect that people have of the Haitian culture, then we are at the same time acknowledging who we are [as African Americans]. Because it is all the same culture; it is all the same language. One of the things that has always been hurtful is that as African Americans, we don't always understand that about our brothers and sisters.[102]

For Godboldo, helping African Americans understand and appreciate Haitian culture is one way to build a sense of pan-African identity and to help Haitians in the United States appreciate the contributions that their country has made to the arts and culture. Godboldo laments that some Haitians do not embrace their own heritage because of the negative stereotypes:

There are a number of Haitians who are not proud of Haitian culture, although many of them have come around. Many did not want to talk about Vodou because it has had such a negative impact on what people have as an impression of Haiti. When they see that I have respect for the culture, they see my [dance] presentation as connecting to a larger African culture, the role that singing and dancing and music play in the lives of all of us. By being involved with Haitian culture here, there has been a reciprocity between us. Sometimes Haitians don't value certain aspects of their culture, which they should. [I want to] let them know that they connect to other black people in the world in a very positive sense. I hope that I have been helping to dispel the myths about Vodou and Haitian folkloric dance and the value of it.[103]

Godboldo also acknowledges that there are many Americans who recoil at the idea of displaying dances that are derived from Vodou ceremonial ritual onstage:

[There are] those who feel that by reproducing aspects of the Vodou ceremony onstage, [it is] frightening. Others feel that it is not advantageous for Africans, African Americans, or Haitians to be seen in that light. What some people are trying to do is to let the world know that we have intellect, that there are aspects of us other than the folkloric material, that we are of this century, that we are intelligent, active people who deserve the respect of the world. Why do we have to have one or the other; why can't we acknowledge both?[104]

Godboldo's challenge to her audiences is to find the commonality of experience between Haitians and non-Haitians: to reach beyond the superficial differences between cultures and celebrate their similarities.

Dance is one tangible cultural activity that allows both Haitians and non-Haitians to embody Haitian culture through movement. Although there are several styles of Haitian dance, most Haitians in Michigan participate in two general styles: social dance and folkloric dance. Social dance is generally practiced at parties and other social events. Although there is a great deal of individual agency in social dance—people are free to pick and choose with whom they will dance—it is usually expected that individuals will dance with different people and that the mood of the event is one of celebration. Social dance is usually done to *mizik konpa* ("popular dance music") and may include several different styles. At a picnic held by Haitians in Belleville, Michigan, on July 4, 2008, a Haitian DJ played a variety of Haitian music, including *konpa,* Haitian rap, and some *mizik rasin* ("roots music"), which borrows its rhythmic patterns from the music of the Vodou ceremony. Children and adults danced together in pairs; for the roots-music selections, they emulated the solo dance style of ceremonial music. Social dance is usually done as a male-female partner dance, although it is common to see women dancing together at an event, especially if there are not enough willing men to serve as partners.

Folkloric dance, on the other hand, is a more specialized form of dance that requires some training in the specific movements and their meanings.

The movements of folkloric dance are based on specific antecedents from Vodou religious ritual. Unlike social dance, in which couples focus their attention on each other, folkloric dance features both solo and large-group dancing with programmatic meanings attached to particular movements. As Kate Ramsey noted in her study of the folkloric movement in Haiti in the 1930s and '40s, Haitian folkloric dance became a popular form of entertainment in Haiti just as the government was cracking down on Vodou practitioners.[105] Since then, Haitians have had conflicted feelings about performing so-called folkloric dance, especially in front of audiences of Americans who may bring their own set of misconceptions to the performance of Haitian culture. For some Haitians, the ambivalence they feel about performing a Vodou-inspired dance makes it a challenge for them to embrace folkloric dancing with enthusiasm.

For many Haitians, however, folkloric dance provides an opportunity to connect with those aspects of Haitian culture that are not readily available outside Haiti. One Detroit Haitian told me that she had attended a performance of Haitian folkloric dance and was interested in finding out more about the cultural significance of specific dance movements. Although she had seen folkloric dance performed many times on video, the experience of physically learning the dance sharpened her appreciation of the dance itself. The Haitian Network Group of Detroit, a cultural organization that promotes Haitian culture in Michigan, has sponsored several public events in which Haitian folkloric dance is performed.

For most people outside Haiti, the visual arts are the most well-known and appreciated aspect of Haitian culture. Since World War II, Haitian painting and sculpture have been valuable commodities on the world art market. Haitian painters such as Louverture Poisson (1914–1984), Castera Bazile (1923–1965), Rigaud Benoît (1911–1986), Gerard Valcin (1923–1988), Hector Hyppolite (1894–1948), and Philomé Obin (1892–1986) are well respected in Haiti and abroad for their original and evocative depictions of Haitian life. In the Detroit area, one of the most outspoken advocates for Haitian art was Roland Wiener, a Haitian art collector who first came to Detroit in 1972 as a lubrication engineer for Mobil Oil and who died in January 2009. According to a 2001 article published in *Krik Krak,* the newsletter of Espoir, a Haitian American cultural organization based in Detroit, Wiener was active in The Friends of African Art (subsequently, the organization changed its name to

Catherine Auguste performing folkloric dance at Corpus Christi Church, Detroit, November 2004. Photo by Bill McNeece.

the Friends of African and African American Art), a group associated with the Detroit Institute of Arts (DIA). In 1982, Wiener and his friend, Haitian ambassador to the United States Georges Léger, suggested that the DIA establish a permanent collection of Haitian art. Wiener, along with his sister, Lina Assad of Haiti, and several others, gathered ninety-six pieces of Haitian art for a special exhibition. The DIA Web site lists eight Haitian paintings on display out of a collection of twenty-seven pieces of Haitian art. According to the article in *Krik Krak*:

> In December 1996, the Friends of African and African American Art recognized and honored Roland [Wiener], who has been on its Board for nearly twenty years, with its prestigious Dr. Alain Locke Award. Named for the noted philosopher who helped launch the era known as the Harlem Renaissance, the award recognizes people who have made an impact on the appreciation of African American culture in the State of Michigan, and whose deeds merit public recognition of their courage and leadership.[106]

Many of the best-known works of Haitian art engage issues of spirituality, a theme that runs throughout the interviews collected for this book. Indeed, most of the Haitians I spoke to commented at length on the importance of their religious beliefs and their desire to worship God in a supportive and welcoming environment. Despite this uniformity of spiritual goals, Haitians participate in a variety of religious communities, most of which are connected to Christianity. The single largest religious denomination among Haitians is Roman Catholicism; as the official religion of Haiti and the most established church in that country, Catholicism has deep roots in Haitian culture. In addition, several Protestant denominations in Michigan serve the needs of Haitians from a variety of religious backgrounds.

For most Haitians, the worship experience provides an opportunity for individuals to meet collectively and to have a meaningful experience that may or may not emphasize Haitian culture. In the Detroit area, most Haitian Catholics worship at Corpus Christi, a new congregation formed when the St. Gerard congregation of northwest Detroit was joined with downtown Detroit's Immaculate Heart of Mary Church. In addition, Haitians worship at Sacred Heart Church and St. Leo Church. In Lansing, the Central Free Methodist Church hosts the Haitian congregation known as the Legliz Méthodiste

Libre du Calvaire (Calvary Free Methodist Church). Led by Haitian pastor Serge Bonhomme, assisted by Beverly Maier, the Calvary Free Methodist Church holds services on Sunday evenings.[107] Like many churches that serve a largely immigrant population, the Haitian congregation shares the Central Free Methodist sanctuary with a larger, predominantly white congregation that holds its worship services on Sunday mornings. Beginning with several praise songs to enliven the congregation and set the spiritual mood for the evening, the service is conducted mostly in Haitian Kreyòl, but Pastor Bonhomme uses Kreyòl, French, and English during his sermons and Bible lessons to keep all congregants—Haitians and Americans alike—engaged in the spirit of the service. On any given Sunday evening, between thirty and forty members may be in attendance; on special occasions such as Christmas, New Year's, and Easter, the number may be closer to eighty.

In Grand Rapids, the Legliz Entènasyonal de Grand Rapids de Nazarean (Grand Rapids West International Church of the Nazarene) is the largest non-Catholic Haitian religious denomination. Led by Pastor Mathieu Pierre, the International Church of the Nazarene averages between fifty and sixty members, with about thirty to forty attending most Sundays. Like the Calvary Haitian church in Lansing, the International Church of the Nazarene features praise music at the beginning of the service, as well as a lively sermon. There is also a bilingual sermon, but in Grand Rapids, unlike Lansing, the pastor preaches in English while one of the musicians from the praise band translates the sermon into Haitian Kreyòl.

Most of the official religious organizations associated with the Haitian community are Christian-based; members are either committed practitioners of Roman Catholicism through a predominantly American congregation or Protestant congregants who attend services given in Haitian Kreyòl. Although several people I spoke to acknowledged that a family member or two practiced Vodou in Haiti, there is relatively little Vodou religious activity in Michigan today. Interest in Haitian traditional religion is, however, very high among diaspora Haitians, especially in the form of cultural programming such as museum exhibitions. One of the most successful such presentations was the "Sacred Arts of Haitian Vodou" exhibition at Detroit's Charles H. Wright Museum of African American History in the fall of 1997. The exhibition brought together a variety of materials, including Vodou ceremonial flags, religious altars, paintings, sculpture, and music; it traveled to art museums and cultural-history museums throughout the United States in the mid-1990s.

According to one Haitian from Detroit, some individuals who publicly denounce Vodou activities may, in fact, be practicing such activities in private. This person went on to say:

> I believe in God, I pray, I love God, but I believe that Vodou exists, too. Something can happen to me; I might feel it. I can't say that I believe [in Vodou], but I might have a little belief all the same. I respect it.[108]

Such respect for the practice of Vodou is easier for Haitians to manage in Michigan than it is back in Haiti, where class prejudice may discourage many middle-class and elite Haitians from participating in Vodou rituals. In Michigan, where the threat of social stigma associated with Vodou practice is not as strong as it is in Haiti, Haitians may have more contact with the symbols, dances, and music of Vodou without risking social ostracism from their neighbors. For example, during a dinner and dance sponsored by Espoir during the week of the "Sacred Arts of Haitian Vodou" exhibit, several Vodou songs were performed. As Haitian psychiatrist Jean Alcé informed me, after two or three songs, six Haitians dancing on the floor became possessed by the spirits simultaneously.[109] Lois Wilcken noted that many Haitians in New York City have an ambivalent relationship with Vodou practice itself but that many people participate in folkloric activities such as dance that are based on movements from the Vodou ceremony.[110] Someone who would never consider attending a ceremony might attend folkloric-dance classes in which they perform the *yanvalou* dance from the Rada denomination of Vodou spirits.[111]

While ambivalence may be the hallmark of most elite and middle-class Haitians attitudes toward Vodou, poorer Haitians, especially those who emigrated to Michigan during the 1990s, have a more complex relationship with Haitian traditional religion. In Lansing, for example, there are many recent immigrants who may have a closer relationship with traditional healing practices than their middle-class neighbors. In a documentary film, *The Haitians, the Healers, and the Anthropologist: Two Case Studies,* anthropologist Philip Singer works with a Puerto Rican *santera,* or spiritual healer, as well as a Native American healer to help two different Haitian immigrants with illnesses they believe required healing by spiritual, not biomedical, means.[112] Singer was asked by a social worker from Lansing's Catholic Social Services to help. The first woman, a Haitian mother of ten children, is visibly distressed; she rocks back and forth and cries throughout the consultation. The second patient, a young Haitian man who complains of burning feet, is unable to work because of his painful condition. In both cases, Singer and his healer associates work with their Haitian patients through an interpreter. The *santera* and the Native American healer improvise spiritual cleansing rituals for each patient—the *santera* ties cloth in knots as a symbol of the patient's spiritual blockage, while the Native American healer uses an eagle feather to wipe away any malevolent spirits from the individuals under treatment—and both patients report an improvement of their symptoms over time. Although Singer's approach to spiritual healing does not directly conform to the rituals of the Vodou ceremony, his patients' willingness to be treated for illnesses they believed to be spiritual is very much in the spirit of healing associated with Vodou.

As this example shows, Haitians are able to adapt to new environments while maintaining connections to their home culture. While the Haitian communities of Michigan may indeed be small, they are also strong in their commitment to Haitian identity and culture.

Haitian Cultural Organizations in Michigan

espite their small numbers, Haitians in Michigan have organized themselves into groups that have made significant contributions to their own community and to the state itself. Bringing together Haitians from different social groups and different generations, Haitian cultural organizations have successfully represented Haitian interests while they have challenged new generations of Haitian Americans to reevaluate their relationship to their home culture. At the dawn of the new century, Haitians continue to promote their culture and heritage while maintaining vital links with other cultural communities in Michigan.

As Chantalle Verna discussed in her study of Haitians in Michigan, several of the earliest cultural organizations in the Haitian community were social in nature. Groups of like-minded Haitians, most of whom were from the same middle-class social background in Haiti, organized parties and celebrations for important holidays, using food and dance as a way to attract Haitian participants.

Verna described several early Haitian organizations that gave local Haitians a place to go and meet other like-minded people. One was Le Baobab, founded in 1982, a "'literary group' that sought to preserve the culture and history of its members' native countries, engage in the news developments back home, and maintain their French."[113] Deriving its name from the large tree found in many parts of western and central Africa, Le Baobab included francophones from Haiti as well as Senegal and other French-speaking parts of Africa.

Another important organization from the 1980s was the Haitian Community Organization of Michigan, or HCOM. According to Verna, HCOM was "founded on October 15, 1984, as a nonprofit organization in an effort to settle a solid base for present and future generations of Haitians living in Michigan. HCOM [proposed], by all possible means, [to] promote Haitian Culture and Art in Michigan."[114] As a predominantly social organization, HCOM sponsored a host of parties, "picnics, raffles, dinner dances, beauty pageants, [and] carnivals."[115]

Espoir: Promoting "Hope" for Haiti from Detroit

Although organizations that identify themselves predominantly as social clubs are an important part of Haitian life in Michigan, some Haitians were interested in founding organizations that dealt with pressing social and political problems within Haiti itself. In the waning days of the Duvalier dictatorship, several Haitians teamed with some African Americans in Detroit to discuss the possibility of starting a Haitian American organization that would help the people of Haiti as they emerged from nearly three decades of totalitarian rule. Choosing the French word for "hope" for their organization's name, the leaders of Espoir "explored ways to aid the Haitian people, as well as to preserve Haiti's proud history and rich culture."[116] When Espoir was founded in 1986, its principal mission was to send much-needed medical supplies to Haiti. With a large population of poor people who had little or no access to health care, Haiti was in desperate need of medicine and primary-care equipment. Between 1990 and 1994, Espoir teamed with Eye Care, a nonprofit organization dedicated to vision care and the prevention of blindness in Haiti. Espoir hosted annual fund-raising events in which Haitian art was auctioned off and the funds generated supported Eye Care's mission.[117] From November 19 to 21, 1993, at Detroit's International Institute, Espoir displayed Haitian art by such internationally well-known Haitian artists as Salnave Philippe-Auguste, Castera Bazile, Rigaud Benoit, Wilson Bigaud, and others.[118]

From 1993 to 2002, Espoir published a quarterly newsletter, *Krik Krak,*

Foreigner, by Jean-Claude Dutès (*Krik Krak*, Fall 1993)

Things are in disarray back home.

Events have thrown me in your midst

As bewildered as a sheep who's gone astray of the herd.

My mind is filled with apprehension.

My vision crowded with fears.

My head resounds with echoes of anticipated pain.

I am lonely.

I am cold.

I am afraid.

I look around me and search for familiar

Faces.

Myriad looks and gazes send me into fright and I shiver with bitterness.

Things are in disarray back home.

And my long lost brothers have spurned me with

the contempt a disdainful host

Reserves for the unwanted guest.

I look around me

Seeking a smile, a look, a gesture

A sign that you are aware of my existence.

Coldly you look through me

Like you would through a clear glass

Of a window on a sunny day.

Not seeing me, not seeing you wither.

Things are in disarray back home.

And I am a long way from home.

which was one of the most important sources of information for Haitians in Michigan and for those interested in supporting the efforts of local Haitians and those abroad. *Krik Krak* took its name from a commonly used phrase to initiate storytelling among rural people in Haiti. When a Haitian story-teller shouts *"Krik!"* to a group of Haitians, the crowd instinctively shouts back, *"Krak!"* The storyteller may then say, *"Tim tim,"* and the audience shouts back, *"Bwa chech!"* and the bond between storyteller and audience is established. By invoking the commonly understood Haitian phrase as the name of the publication, the members of Espoir indicated that they had a responsibility to their audience to provide them with edifying and entertain-ing information about their world.[119]

One of Espoir's projects in Haiti itself has been promoting reforestation, one of the most serious environmental threats to Haitian well-being. Most of the trees in Haiti have been cut down for use as charcoal for cooking fuel. In 1991, Espoir sponsored a fact-finding mission to Haiti to "study deforestation and environmental restoration."[120]

Espoir has also been active in promoting community awareness of the concerns of Haitians both in Haiti and in the United States. From 1991 to 1993, for example, students from law schools around the country began donating their time and skills to help Haitian refugees apply for political asylum in the United States. Espoir helped connect seventeen students from the University of Michigan Law School to this nationwide effort and sent them to be trained at the Haitian Refugee Center in Miami. Most of the clients helped by this ef-fort were in Lansing, Michigan. Law students gathered personal information from each of the asylum seekers, ensuring that the important "addendum" to their asylum application demonstrated that they were, indeed, in danger of political persecution if they were returned to Haiti.[121]

In addition to its own efforts to help Haitians in Michigan, Espoir has promoted different aspects of Haitian life through cultural programming and criticism. From 1986 until 2000, Espoir hosted an annual banquet that often included presentations of Haitian music and dance. For example, at the ninth annual Espoir banquet at the Westin Hotel on November 19, 1994, Haitian dancer Louines Louinis joined Professor Penny Godboldo of Marygrove Col-lege for a dance performance that included a *bal chanpèt* ("rural dance") and an invocation to Legba, a Haitian Vodou spirit who serves as the guardian of the gate between the material and spiritual worlds. Louinis has made several

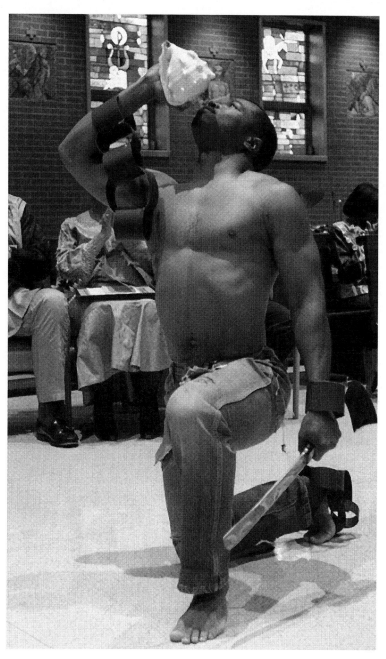

Haitian dancer Maxceau Cylla poses as the nèg mawon, *or runaway slave, at Corpus Christi Church, Detroit, November 2004. Photo by Bill McNeece.*

visits to the Detroit area, mostly to teach at the annual Summer School of the Performing Arts at Marygrove College.[122] Another important dancer who has shared her talents with the Detroit Haitian community is Paulette St.-Lot, the founder of the Ibo Dancers and an attaché at the Organization of African Unity for the United Nations. St.-Lot and her husband, Henri Franck, who was the director of the Haitian Neighborhood Service Center in Brooklyn, New York, have performed several times for Espoir's annual banquets. Maxceau Cylla, a Haitian dancer who settled in Detroit, also performs locally for cultural functions.

In 1991, Espoir, the Charles H. Wright Museum of African American History in Detroit, and the National Afro-American Museum and Cultural Center in Wilberforce, Ohio, cosponsored an exhibition of more than eighty art works that depicted Haiti's historic slave revolt. Titled "A Battle of Titans: The Slave Revolution in the Americas," the exhibition commemorated the start of the 1791–1804 Haitian Revolution, which marked the beginning of the end of slavery in the Americas.

Another successful collaboration between Espoir and the greater Detroit arts community was the "Sacred Arts of Haitian Vodou" exhibition held at the Charles H. Wright Museum of African American History from October 10 to December 21, 1997.[123] The exhibition, which featured more than 500 pieces, including Haitian paintings, iron work, sculpture, and ceremonial objects from the Vodou ceremony, was prepared by the Fowler Museum of Cultural History at the University of California at Los Angeles.[124]

In conjunction with the Alfred Berkowitz Art Gallery at the University of Michigan at Dearborn, Espoir sponsored an exhibition titled "200 Zan Libète/200 Years of Freedom/200 Ans de Liberté," which ran from January 12 to February 6, 2004. The exhibition was in observance of the 200th anniversary of Haitian independence and featured a presentation by Wayne State University professor of anthropology Guérin Montilus, "Ancestral Memory, Vision, and Struggle in Haitian Art." According to Claude Jacobs, an associate professor of behavioral sciences at the University of Michigan at Dearborn (UMD), the exhibition "allows us to observe the successful liberation efforts led by Toussaint Louverture two centuries ago while affirming our commitment to critically examining the various cultures of people of African descent around the world."[125] UMD sociology professor William McNeece provided a collection of documentary photos of Haitian cultural artifacts to accompany the exhibition.

As a Haitian American group founded to promote Caribbean culture within Michigan, Espoir has collaborated with other groups in the state to provide cultural programming that would be of interest to a wide range of citizens. In 2001, Espoir joined forces with the Africana Studies Department at Wayne State University and with the Charles H. Wright Museum of African American History to sponsor "A Tribute to the Fight for Social Revolution: The 100 Year Anniversary Celebration of the Birth of C. L. R. James." James, a scholar from Trinidad and author of *The Black Jacobins: Toussaint L'Ouverture and the San Domingo Revolution,* one of the most widely admired books on the Haitian Revolution, was an important Caribbean intellectual who "played an active part in democratic movements in the West Indies and Africa."[126] The James celebration included six lectures by visiting academics from the University of Southern California, Brown University, Loyola Marymount University, Marymount Manhattan College, and Western Michigan University.[127]

Espoir also sponsored a "Prelude to the Celebration of the Bicentennial of the Independence of Haiti" on May 18, 2002 at the Institute of Metropolitan Detroit.[128] Haiti's status as a free black nation has been a consistent source of pride for contemporary Haitians, and they proudly display their culture in connection with this solemn anniversary. The program featured a lecture by Marc Christophe of the University of the District of Columbia on Toussaint Louverture, one of the Haitian generals who fought the French during the revolution. Geraud Dimanche, a well-known Haitian drummer in the Detroit area, provided a recital of Haitian drumming styles. Karen Dimanche Davis, an anthropologist at Detroit's Marygrove College, moderated a panel on the experiences of Haitians in the diaspora.

Although Espoir was founded to highlight the achievements of Haitians in the United States and abroad, the group has also been active in promoting the successes of other people from the Caribbean whose contributions to American culture are also regularly overlooked. Espoir has had a long-standing commitment to reach out to Cubans and Puerto Ricans in an effort to highlight their shared concerns as Caribbean people. During a meeting sponsored by the Justice for Cuba Coalition on February 12, 2000, several members of Espoir "heard from a number of speakers expressing their solidarity with Cuba, not only regarding efforts to end the current stand-off, but toward ending the U.S. embargo and normalizing relations with the island nation."[129] The meeting was prompted by the Elian Gonzalez affair in which a Cuban refugee living in southern Florida was the subject of a custody battle between his anti-Castro relatives in the United States and his father, who was a resident of Cuba. Although Gonzalez was eventually returned to Cuba to be with his father, there was a lengthy stand-off between Cuban Americans in Florida and the U.S. authorities. Public opinion on the Castro regime varies widely among Haitians in the United States, but most Haitians saw an inequity in the way Gonzalez, a citizen of Cuba, was treated in comparison with most Haitian refugees in the United States. In September 2000, Espoir's newsletter contrasted the expedience of Gonzalez's case with that of six-year-old Sophonie Telcy, a Haitian asylum seeker whose mother died shortly after arriving in the United States with her family.[130] Telcy's tragic case barely registered in the national news, while Gonzalez was front-page fare for several weeks in all major U.S. newspapers and television markets.

Espoir's interest in young people is not limited to those who make national headlines. The organization sponsored an essay contest for several years that rewarded Detroit-area high school and first-year college students for essays that "promote cultural, historical, and political understanding of the Caribbean."[131] The second place winner of the 1993 Espoir essay contest was Timothy Tewawn Sylvester, a Martin Luther King High School student, who died of an illness shortly after winning the award. His essay on Toussaint Louverture was written from the point of view of Toussaint's son. The 1994 scholarship essay winner was Sabriya Avington, a senior at Renaissance High School in Detroit, who wrote her essay about Jamaican political and religious leader Marcus Garvey.

Espoir's work as a Haitian American organization cultivating connections among people from all over the Caribbean led several of its early founders to seek a permanent home for the group. After several years of fund-raising and searching for an appropriate property, Espoir purchased a historic home at 421 East Ferry Street near downtown Detroit and in 1998 opened the Espoir Center for Caribbean Arts and Culture (CCAC). CCAC operated for several years, but the property was sold in 2004. Since then, Espoir has scaled back many of its cultural activities, but other organizations have begun promoting Haitian and Caribbean culture in the area.

Toussaint Louverture, by Timothy Sylvester
(*Krik Krak*, Fall 1993)

On August 11, 1791, a meeting was held by the blacks, under the guise of a Voodoo ceremony, to plan a revolt against the French domination of Haiti. It was a dark and dreary night; the sky was black as ebony and the stars shone like diamonds. The wind whistled through the air as everyone gathered at their respective places for the surprise attack. I was very young at the time of the revolt, but I noticed a burning fire in the eyes of everyone who had gathered at the meeting place; the men were full of excitement and courage. The day had finally come when the whiteman would have to bow.

It was just after ten o'clock on the night of August the 22nd when the drum beat rang into the air with a clatter. I looked at my father as he ran from the hut, and he turned and said, Tonight my son shall be free to grow strong and brave as a man should, and he turned and grabbed his weapons and ran to meet the others. Many did die that night of the 22nd of August, but they died for the freedom of all. I was too young to understand everything that occurred on that night, but I was told by my mother that I was the son of a great warrior who would bathe his son in a fresh new freedom. No longer would it be just a sprinkle, but it would be like a river overrunning its banks. Thus began a new day for many of our people; we had overcome many odds and fought against the best outfit that the enemy could send us, and we won.

I was the son of a great leader who had the power to inspire his men with a sense of revolutionary fervor and a deep sincere belief in the cause of freedom. He used the power of words to empower his men with the strength to fight, which led to our great triumph of victory. Toussaint Louverture led his people through a very trying insurrection which led to our freedom.

Haitian Network Group of Detroit

Perhaps the most active of the current Haitian organizations in Michigan is the Haitian Network Group of Detroit (HNGD). Created in July 1998, HNGD was founded by Fritz Momplaisir, Marie Soledad Nelson, and Margareth Pierre Corkery, "with the intent to promote Haitian culture and provide an

Claire Danjou and Margareth Corkery working at an HNGD fund-raising dinner, February 2007. Photo by Bill McNeece.

environment for Haitians and friends to network." Founded as a cultural organization, HNGD does not pursue any particular political ideology. Instead, the group provides "a forum where Haitians in the area would exchange ideas, discuss current events and network."[132] HNGD has been very active in recent years with a series of programs designed to connect local Haitians with important cultural activities and to inform non-Haitian audiences about cultural and social issues related to Haiti.

One of HNGD's earliest efforts to bring a Haitian cultural performance to Detroit audiences was the June 2002 performance of *Lea Kokoye*, a staged dramatic reading of a play by famed Haitian storyteller and dramatist Maurice Sixto. Sixto's work draws upon Haitian proverbs, folklore, and other meaningful aspects of Haitian culture; his work is very funny, but the themes he traces often connect to deeper Haitian cultural issues that are serious in nature. In an effort to explain Sixto's work to non-Haitian audiences, HNGD sponsored a cultural program in 2006 titled "Spend an Afternoon with Maurice Sixto" and conducted a roundtable discussion of some of the major themes in Sixto's work.[133]

From November 5 to 7, 2004, HNGD sponsored "1804—Celebrating a Legacy—2004," to commemorate the 200th anniversary of Haitian independence. Held at the Charles H. Wright Museum of African American History, the program featured a lecture by Marc Christophe on "Decoding the Haitian Flag: Symbols and Symbolism," as well as a series of workshops. Adeline Auguste and Elizabeth James led a session on Haitian storytelling; Geraud Dimanche and Maxceau Cylla ran workshops on drumming and dancing, respectively; and Gilbert Targette provided a session on Haitian games.[134]

HNGD has also brought films about Haiti and Haitian filmmakers to Detroit for a film festival at Detroit's Arab American Museum. "Eyes on Haiti: The Reel Deal" was held on October 15 and October 22, 2006, and featured four films that explore the Haitian experience in Haiti and the United States. *Haitian Eksperyans* (directed by David Belle) explores "Haiti's rich history and shows the world that Haiti has much to offer." Director Robin Lloyd's *Haiti Rising: Black Dawn* uses animation to depict a Caribbean folktale, and her *Haiti Rising: Haitian Pilgrimage* follows a Haitian American family from Boston as they return to Haiti to trace their ancestral roots. Finally, Sacha Parisot's *La Rebelle* is a fictional account of a "sweet Haitian girl [who] becomes a foul-mouthed, alcohol-drinking, drug-taking, promiscuous teen

Lyrics to "La Dessalinienne," the Haitian national anthem; music by Nicholas Fénélon Geffrard, words by Justin Lhérisson

Pour le Pays, pour les Ancêtres,
Marchons unis, Marchons unis.
Dans nos rangs point de traîtres!
Du sol soyons seuls maîtres.
Marchons unis, Marchons unis
Pour le Pays, pour les Ancêtres,
Marchons, marchons, marchons unis,
Pour le Pays, pour les Ancêtres.

Pour les Aïeux, pour la Patrie
Béchons joyeux, béchons joyeux
Quand le champ fructifie
L'âme se fortifie
Béchons joyeux, béchons joyeux
Pour les Aïeux, pour la Patrie
Béchons, béchons, béchons joyeux
Pour les Aïeux, pour la Patrie

Pour le Pays et pour nos Pères
Formons des Fils, formons des Fils
Libres, forts et prospères

Toujours nous serons frères
Formons des Fils, formons des Fils
Pour le Pays et pour nos Pères.
Formons, formons, formons des Fils
Pour le Pays et pour nos Pères.

Pour les Aïeux, pour la Patrie
O Dieu des Preux, O Dieu des Preux
Sous ta garde infinite
Prends nos droits, notre vie
O Dieu des Preux, O Dieu des Preux
Pour les Aïeux, pour la Patrie.
O Dieu, O Dieu, O Dieu des Preux
Pour les Aïeux, pour la Patrie.

Pour le Drapeau, pour la Patrie
Mourir est beau, mourir est beau!
Notre passé nous crie:
Ayez l'âme aguerrie!
Mourir est beau, mourir est beau
Pour le Drapeau, pour la Patrie.

when she finds her single dad with a new girlfriend."[135] The festival brought the sights and sounds of Haiti to local audiences and gave community members an opportunity to respond to the films. On October 15, Karen Dimanche Davis, associate professor and chair of humanities at Marygrove College in Detroit, provided comments on *Haitian Eksperyans* and *Haiti Rising*. On October 22, Sacha Parisot led a discussion about his own *La Rebelle*.[136]

In addition to their work to promote Haiti through public programming,

Mourir, mourir, mourir est beau
Pour le Drapeau, pour la Patrie.

For our country, for our ancestors,
United let us march.
Let there be no traitors in our ranks!
Let us be masters of our soil.
United let us march
For our country, for our ancestors.
March, march, march united
For the country, for the ancestors.

For our forebears, for our country
Let us toil joyfully
May the fields be fertile
And our souls take courage.
Let us toil joyfully
For our forebears, for our country.
Toil, toil, toil joyfully
For our forebears, for our country.

For our country, for our forefathers,
Let us train our sons.
Free, strong, and prosperous,
We shall always be as brothers.

Let us train our sons
For our country and for our
  forefathers.
Train, train, train our sons
For the country and for our
  forefathers.

For our forebears, for our country,
Oh God of the valiant!
Take our rights and our life
Under your infinite protection,
Oh God of the valiant
For our forebears, for our country.
Oh God, O God, O God of the valiant
For our forebears, for the country.

For the flag, for our country
To die is a fine thing!
Our past cries out to us:
Have a disciplined soul!
To die is a fine thing,
For the flag, for our country.
Death, death, death is beautiful
For the flag, for the country

the members of HNGD also sponsor events that draw on Haitian culture in different ways. For several years, HNGD has sponsored "L'Ajoupa," a celebration every August that features Haitian cuisine, storytelling, and other activities designed to make Haitian culture come alive for Haitians in the diaspora and non-Haitians alike. An *ajoupa* (or *joupa*) is a one-room hut with a thatched roof, unplastered latticework walls, and a dirt floor that is most often found in the Haitian countryside. Although most of the Haitians

Haitian Network Group of Detroit's "1804—Celebrating a Legacy—2004" program cover.

living in Detroit have never lived in a *joupa* in Haiti, the structure itself evokes Haitian rural life in its natural beauty and emphasis on community collaboration. HNGD members construct a small *joupa* for each celebration and go to great lengths to supply the small house with items that evoke Haitian rural life. Margareth Corkery, a former board member of HNGD, told me that one year, event organizers decided to use a *lanp tètgridap,* a small oil lamp made from a tin can and without a glass chimney, as a way to remind participants of their Haitian roots. *Lanp tètgridap* translates literally as "lamp with kinky hair," a reference to the woolly wick that sticks out of the top; such lamps are found all over the Haitian countryside, used by thousands of rural merchants throughout Haiti and in cities in western Africa. Corkery told me that HNGD members tried to import several *lanp tètgridap* from Miami but were forced

Haitian Network Group of Detroit's "Eyes on Haiti: The Reel Deal" film festival program cover, October 2006.

to turn to a fellow Haitian in Grand Rapids who happened to have some of the lamps in her possession.[137] Through their efforts to create a Haitian environment in Michigan, members of HNGD reaffirm their connection to Haitian culture and to their fellow Haitians.

Like Espoir, HNGD has worked with organizations in Haiti to promote education, health care, and quality of life for Haitians living in poverty. It has also cooperated with other groups in Michigan to promote education for rural Haitians. For example, in the HNGD newsletter, *Zanmi Detroit* ("Detroit Friends"), Julie Fleming described the Pichon Project, in which the Peace Education Center in East Lansing, Michigan, sponsors an ele-mentary-school program and a microcredit program for women to establish small businesses that will benefit families in Haiti. Headed by East Lansing

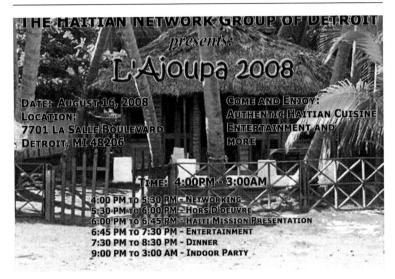

THE HAITIAN NETWORK GROUP OF DETROIT
presents:

L'Ajoupa 2008

DATE: AUGUST 16, 2008   COME AND ENJOY:
LOCATION: AUTHENTIC HAITIAN CUISINE
7701 LA SALLE BOULEVARD   ENTERTAINMENT AND
DETROIT, MI 48206   MORE

TIME: 4:00PM - 3:00AM

4:00 PM TO 5:30 PM - NETWORKING
5:30 PM TO 6:00 PM - HORS D'OEUVRE
6:00 PM TO 6:45 PM - HAITI MISSION PRESENTATION
6:45 PM TO 7:30 PM - ENTERTAINMENT
7:30 PM TO 8:30 PM - DINNER
9:00 PM TO 3:00 AM - INDOOR PARTY

Flyer advertising the Haitian Network Group of Detroit's annual L'Ajoupa celebration,
August 2008.

educator Pierre Balthazar, the Pichon Project has also tried to bring solar
technology to families as a way to curb the use of charcoal and thus slow the
rate of deforestation in Haiti.[138]

Caribbean Carnival and Cultural Organization

While Espoir and the Haitian Network Group of Detroit were founded to ad-
dress issues that affect the Haitian American community in Michigan, other
groups include Haitians in a larger, pan-Caribbean network. The Caribbean Carnival and Cultural Organization (CCCO), formed in 1979, brought
people living in Detroit from several different Caribbean nations together
in order "to promote and interpret Caribbean culture to the Metropolitan
Detroit community through educational means and cultural activities; to
promote greater cooperation and unity among Caribbean people living
in the Metropolitan Detroit area, and to highlight the bringing together of
Caribbean people in a major annual event, a Caribbean Festival, termed
'CARIVAL' in August."[139] *Carival* is an adaptation of "Carnival," a seasonal
celebration that occurs during the last few days before Lent in the Christian
liturgical calendar. During Carnival, celebrants anticipate the deprivation

of the Lenten season by taking to the streets, using exuberant dances and songs to express themselves. In Detroit's Carival, members of different local Caribbean communities come together to sponsor a parade in which costumed celebrants dance to recorded music performed from flat-bed trucks. There is also a series of concerts of different types of Caribbean music, as well as Miss Carival and Junior Miss Carival pageants in which contestants compete for scholarships by performing talents and demonstrating skills at public speaking. As the CCCO program from 2001 states, "The Junior Miss Carival and Miss Carival Pageants are not beauty pageants. They are among the activities of the Caribbean Community which provide our youth opportunities for cultural experiences."[140] Each year, a different country is featured in the Carival celebration. In 2001, Barbados was the featured country; 2008 celebrated Guyana's cultural heritage.

There is a lively Carnival tradition in Haiti, but Haitians are outnumbered in the Detroit community by Trinidadians, who embrace Carnival as a national pastime. Nevertheless, Haitians participate in Carival regularly; Marie-José Alcé, a longtime resident of Detroit, has served on CCCO for twenty years. For Carival 2007, Danielle Desroches dressed in a Trinidadian-style Carnival costume and paraded with her fellow Caribbeans on the streets around Hart Plaza in downtown Detroit.

Putting aside cultural differences and coming together as Caribbean-descended people, at least for a short time every August, Haitians can affirm their own culture and the cultures of their Caribbean neighbors.

Haiti Outreach Mission

For some Haitians who have come to settle in the United States, the plight of those in Haiti who lack basic medical care weighs heavily on them. As a country without basic medical services available for most of the population, Haiti depends on foreign aid for much of its heath care for the rural poor. Haitians and non-Haitians from the United States have been active in bringing basic medical care to rural Haitians, sponsoring regular medical missions to Haiti that provide fluoride treatments for children's teeth and clinics for primary care.

In 1998, Dominique Mondé-Matthews, a Haitian-born pediatrician, and her American husband, Roger Matthews, founded the Haiti Outreach

Danielle Desroches participates in Detroit's Carival celebration, August 2007. Photo by Michael Largey.

Adeline Auguste addresses Haitian churchgoers during a visit of the Haiti Outreach Mission to Mirebalais, Haiti, June 2005. Photo by Bill McNeece.

Mission (HOM), an ecumenical lay mission group drawing from Episcopal, Catholic, and Baptist members, among others. HOM travels to Mirebalais, Haiti, every spring to provide a weeklong medical clinic for local residents. HOM is made up of Haitian and non-Haitian volunteers from all over Michigan. Although the group was first affiliated with St. Gerard Catholic Church of Detroit and St. David's Episcopal Church of Southfield, other Michigan churches, including Holy Cross of Novi, Our Lady of Victory in Northville, St. Blaise in Sterling Heights, and All Saints Episcopal in East Lansing, have joined with HOM to provide medical volunteers and nonspecialist workers for the project. HOM works with two local churches in Mirebalais: St. Louis Catholic Church and St. Pierre Episcopal Church. HOM's commitment to Mirebalais includes not only a medical clinic (which is supported year-round by donations from HOM) but also construction work for a school, a dental clinic, an orphanage and a bakery.[141]

For many Haitians who have made the mission trip to Mirebalais, the chance to give back to their Haitian compatriots is a powerful experience. Mondé-Matthews told me of one health-care provider who traveled with HOM to Mirebalais to serve as a translator for one of the physicians. The woman told Mondé-Matthews that she couldn't believe she had waited so long to go back. She added, "This is something important; we have to give back."[142] Mondé-Matthews herself explained that returning to Haiti to provide medical care "shows that we can still give something of our own; we can show [the people of Mirebalais] that we are not afraid of them, we understand their suffering, and that we can make a difference in their lives."[143]

Danielle Desroches, a registered nurse who has made the trip to Mirebalais seven times, told me, "It is hard to explain my feelings about the mission trip. I didn't think that I would carry those people back with me. . . . I feel honored to be a part of the mission team; we help people help themselves."[144]

Through their active civic and cultural organizations in Michigan, Haitians maintain contact not only with their immediate families but also with a vast number of Haitians across the social spectrum in Haiti. Like many other diaspora Haitians in the United States, the Haitians of Michigan participate in a transnational experience of being Haitian, bringing their resources and expertise to other Haitians here and abroad.

Conclusion

In Michigan, Haitians have adapted to a new way of life while maintaining vital connections to Haiti and its people. They have created social and religious organizations that sustain their culture as they work with their non-Haitian neighbors to make Michigan a better place to live. Haitians make an impact on Michigan life in professions ranging from the medical and business communities to the unskilled labor force. During the height of the Duvalier dictatorship from the 1960s to the 1980s, many Haitian immigrants living in the United States despaired of ever having a chance to see their native land again. With the downfall of the dictatorship and the reestablishment of democratic rule in Haiti, many Haitians—from professionals to minimum-wage earners—have returned to Haiti in order to share some of their own resources with friends and family members.

Since the downfall of the Aristide administration in 2005, the political situation in Haiti has deteriorated, leaving many Haitians in Michigan concerned about the future of their ancestral homeland. During difficult times like these, Haitians abroad become an even more important support system for those living in Haiti, either by sending money in the form of remittances, or by participating in medical or educational missions to rural Haiti in order to bring badly needed resources to local communities.

On January 12, 2010, an earthquake that registered 7.0 on the Richter scale struck Haiti. The epicenter of the temblor was less than twenty miles from Port-au-Prince, where more than two million Haitians live. Since few buildings in the city were constructed according to earthquake-resistant building codes, many of the structures in Port-au-Prince and surrounding towns fell down, trapping people under mounds of broken concrete. As this book goes to press, the final death toll is unknown, but estimates put the loss of life somewhere around 200,000 people, and an additional million people injured or homeless. Most of the landmarks of Port-au-Prince were damaged or destroyed; the Presidential Palace or Palais National collapsed, as did most of the government buildings in the center of the city. The Roman Catholic Cathedral a few blocks away was leveled, as was the Holy Trinity Episcopal Cathedral, home of several famous murals painted by Haitian artists during the 1950s. The painting behind the altar in Holy Trinity Cathedral—a black, crucified Christ that looked benevolently over his Haitian brothers and sisters—was reduced to a pile of rubble in a matter of minutes.

Haitians in Michigan have been quick to respond to the catastrophe in Haiti by organizing events that have kept people informed about the situation in the country and by raising money for earthquake relief. For example, on February 19, 2010, the Haitian Community of Michigan and the Penny Godboldo Institute sponsored a Haiti Earthquake Victims Memorial that featured a remembrance for the earthquake victims by Margareth Corkery, a presentation on Haitian resiliency by Haitian psychologist Jean-Claude Dutès, and a discussion of the significance of Haitian culture by Penny Godboldo. In addition, the Haitian community paid special tribute to Roger Matthews, co-founder of Haiti Outreach Mission, who died suddenly on January 24, 2010. Although Matthews's connection to Haiti was originally through his marriage to Haitian physician Dominique Mondé-Matthews, his love for Haiti and its people made him a cherished member of Detroit's Haitian community.

In February 2010, Michigan social services providers prepared to receive Haitian survivors of the earthquake. Just as their predecessors came to Michigan sixteen years earlier as political refugees from Haiti's military junta–led regime, a new wave of Haitians will migrate to Lansing, Grand Rapids, and Detroit in search of a better life. Haitians who are already in Michigan will welcome their countrymen and begin the process of rebuilding their shared homeland.

Although the Haitian population of Michigan is not large in comparison to those of Arab, German, or Dutch ancestry, Haitians in Michigan are an important part of the cultural mosaic of life in the state. Their contributions to the community are large in proportion to their relatively small size.

Appendix 1

Internet Resources on Haiti

There are many Internet sites that feature information about Haiti and about Haitians living in the United States. The following are some popular Web sites that deal with Haitian subjects.

General Information about Haitians in the United States

Http://ccde.umb.edu/summerinstitute/haitiancreole: University of Massachusetts, Boston, Haitian Creole Summer Institute.

Www.everyculture.com/multi/Du-Ha/Haitian-Americans.html: History of Haitians in the United States.

Www.haitianinternet.com: Social networking site for Haitians.

Www.haitianstudies.umb.edu: Haitian Studies Association.

Www.haitiantreasures.com/HT_haitian_flag.day1.htm: Haitian Flag Day information.

Www.haiti-usa.org/index.php: History of Haitians in the United States, with a section on Detroit.

Www.indiana.edu/~creole/haitiancreole.html: Indiana University Creole Institute, Bloomington.

Www.miamigov.com/haiti2004/magic.htm: City of Miami's Haitian community.

Www.sakapfet.com: Social networking site for Haitians in the United States, Haiti, and elsewhere.

Haitian Cultural Organizations

Www.chicagocarifete.com: Chicago Caribbean Carnival Association.
Www.haitiancongress.com: Haitian Congress to Fortify Haiti, Chicago.
Www.hngd.com: Haitian Network Group of Detroit.
Www.makandal.org: La Troupe Makandal, New York's Center for Haitian Drum and Dance.
Www.myccco.com: Caribbean Cultural and Carnival Organization, Detroit.

Haitian Radio Stations

Www.anselme.homestead.com/RADIO.html: List of Haitian radio stations in the United States.
Www.radiolumiere.org: Radio Lumiere, Haiti.
Www.radiopanou.com: Radio Pa Nou, Haiti.
Www.radiosoleil.com: Radio Soleil, Haiti.
Www.radiotriomphe.com: Radio Triomphe Internationale.

Haitian Newspapers

Www.haitienmarche.com: Haiti en Marche.
Www.haiti-observateur.com: Haiti Observateur.
Www.haitiprogres.com: Haiti Progres.
Www.haitiantimes.com: Haitian Times.

Churches with Haitian Affiliations

Www.centralfreemethodist.org: Calvary Haitian Church, Lansing, Mich.
Www.corpuschristi-detroit.org: Corpus Christi Church, Detroit.
Www.sacredheartdetroit.com: Sacred Heart Church, Detroit.

Michigan Relief Organizations Working in Haiti

Www.haitioutreachmission.org: Haiti Outreach Mission, Southfield, Mich.

Www.raysofhopeforhaiti.com: Rays of Hope for Haiti, Grand Rapids, Mich.

Appendix 2

Haitian Language

Most Haitians, with the exception of some people born outside Haiti, speak Haitian Creole or *kreyòl ayisyen* (or Kreyòl, as I refer to it here). Taking its name from the word *creole* which refers to a type of mixture or fusion, Kreyòl has been spoken in Haiti since the early days of the Saint-Domingue colony. Creole languages are the result of large-scale contact between distinct language communities. Most often, contact languages known as pidgins initially form as trade languages between different language communities. When the pidgin language becomes the native language of a specific group, that language is said to be a creole language. In the case of Kreyòl, Africans and Europeans had extensive contact through the slave economies of the western hemisphere. In fact, *kreyòl ayisyen* has moved beyond the creole designation to become an independent language in its own right, but the name Creole has remained, reminding Haitians of their complex linguistic history. Some Haitians also speak French, but they are mostly middle- and upper-class people who live in urban areas in the country. The vast majority of Haitians in Haiti speak only Kreyòl.

Most of the vocabulary for Kreyòl comes from the French colonial influence in the late seventeenth through the eighteenth centuries. Despite the heavy borrowing of nouns and verbs from French, Kreyòl syntax is different from French, making it unintelligible to native French speakers. Many

Kreyòl nouns that are derived from French words retain the article associated with that word. For example:

FRENCH		KREYÒL
La ville (the town)	becomes	*Lavil* (town)

Notice that the Kreyòl word loses the article *the* when transformed from French. In order to make the Kreyòl word *lavil* mean "*the* town," it is necessary to add an article to the end of the word. For example:

Lavil (town)
Lavil la (the town)

Although many nouns retain their gender associations from French, the personal pronouns in Kreyòl are not gendered. The third-person pronoun *li* refers to he, she, or it. The personal pronouns in Kreyòl are:

I: *mwen* or *m*	we: *nou*
you: *ou* or *w*	you (plural): *nou*
he/she/it: *li*	they: *yo*

Notice that the first- and second-person plural pronouns (we and you plural) are the same in Kreyòl.

Verbs in Kreyòl are not formally conjugated; instead, verb tenses are indicated by the presence of verb markers that tell the listener when something has happened. For example, the verb *manje* (to eat) can be used in the following ways.

KREYÒL	ENGLISH
Mwen manje	I ate or I eat
M ap manje	I am eating
M te manje	I ate something (and am done eating)
M ta manje	I would eat
M a manje	I will eat

In each case, the verb *manje* is unchanged when the verb tense changes.

Also note that when verb markers are added, the personal pronoun *mwen* contracts to the short form *m*.

Kreyòl is a language that is rich in proverbial expressions. Such expressions are used by individuals in everyday speech to convey a deep understanding of a situation. The following are some common Haitian proverbs:

Pale franse pa di lespri pou sa. (To be able to speak French doesn't make you intelligent.) Only middle- and upper-class Haitians speak French, so this proverb aims a subtle criticism at upper-class snobbery about lower-class Haitians.

Youn sèl dwet pa ka manje kalalou. (A single finger can't eat okra.) People must cooperate to accomplish something.

Pitit se richès pou malerè. (Children are wealth for the poor.)

Before 1979, there was no official orthography or writing system for Kreyòl, so authors interested in writing in the language were forced to make their own transliterations of Kreyòl or to adapt one of several orthographies. In 1979, the Haitian government adopted an official orthography for Kreyòl and made it a "national" language in Haiti; until that time, French was the official language of government and business. Now, many government functions including the courts are conducted in Kreyòl so that monolingual Kreyòl speakers can participate in civic life more easily.

Common Words

yes: *wi*	no: *non*
man: *msye*	woman: *madanm*
boy: *gason*	girl: *fi*
child: *timoun*	good: *bon*
big: *gwo*	small: *piti*
water: *dlo*	sun: *solèy*
fish: *pwason*	bird: *zwazo*
dog: *chen*	tree: *pyebwa*
three: *twa*	

Common Phrases

Ki jan w ye?	How are you?
Mwen byen, mèsi.	I'm fine, thank you.
Kouman moun yo ye?	How's your family?
	(Literally, "How are the people?")
Kote w prale?	Where are you going?
Mwen prale nan mache a.	I'm going to the market.

Learning Kreyòl

People interested in learning Kreyòl have several options. There are summer programs available to study Kreyòl in the United States, the most popular of which are the Indiana Creole Institute at Indiana University in Bloomington and the Haitian Creole Summer Institute at the University of Massachusetts in Boston. Indiana's Creole Institute sells both a Haitian-English dictionary and a textbook, *Ann Pale Kreyòl: An Introductory Course in Haitian Creole,* which has ten supplemental CDs with exercises and pronunciation models. Finally, Bryant Freeman from the University of Kansas has published a Haitian Creole-English dictionary that is available at www.amazon.com.

Appendix 3

Flavors of Haiti

Two plump, whole red snappers sizzled in the skillet. A bowl of conch in Creole sauce waited in the dining room. Pans of cassava pudding cooled on the counter. And puff-pastry appetizers stuffed with spicy ground meat filled a pan near the stove. But the cooking was far from finished.

By the time Marie Jose Alcé and her dinner party guests would finally sit down to eat, she would have prepared more than a dozen traditional and special-occasion Haitian dishes, in quantities large enough to feed two or three times the number of people around the table. Haiti may suffer from poverty and political problems, but its rich culinary heritage and its traditions of sharing are a source of pride in metro Detroit's Haitian community.

It's hard to imagine a home cook more skillful with the country's flavors and ingredients than Alcé (pronounced ahl-SAY), whose home in Detroit's Palmer Woods neighborhood is a gathering spot for friends and friends-of-friends. And on this recent Saturday afternoon, some who weren't even coming for dinner were dropping in.

They'd heard about the marvelous repast she was preparing for a visiting food writer and were good-naturedly volunteering to take the leftovers off

Sylvia Rector, "Flavors of Haiti: Culture and Cuisine Combine in the Island Nation's Unique Cuisine," *Detroit Free Press*, April 16, 2002: 1F, 2F. Reprinted by permission of the *Detroit Free Press*.

her hands. With no Haitian restaurants in metro Detroit, authentic tastes of the island nation are hard to find—whether you're looking for good home cooking or a glimpse into an unfamiliar cuisine. But Alcé's kitchen provided both.

If you could taste the food and listen to her and others talk about Haiti's food traditions and vivid flavors, you'd learn about fish, fiery peppers, exotic fruits and vegetables, and *riz et pois,* the national dish of rice and beans. You'd also learn how history, geography and economics have shaped the cuisine, and how different one Caribbean country's food can be from another's.

"People don't know about Haiti's food until they go there," says Alcé, who was born in Haiti and owns the Joe-Mar Travel Agency in Oak Park. "But everybody who goes says the same thing—that Haiti's food is very, very good. They come back and they keep talking about the food."

Seasoned by Circumstance

A shared geography gives Caribbean cuisines many similarities. From Nassau and the Bahamas in the north to Trinidad and Tobago in the southeast, Caribbean cooks use an abundance of fish and shellfish and the region's tropical fruits, vegetables and root crops—coconuts, plantains, mangos, limes, okra, rice, beans, peas, yams and cassava, among others.

But history seasons Caribbean food with a heavy hand, as well.

Africans enslaved to work in the sugar cane plantations brought their dietary and cooking traditions with them to the islands. And the European countries—mostly England, Spain and France—that controlled different groups of islands also left indelible marks on the territories they ruled.

"You can see the influence of the dominating countries in everything from language to food," says Guerda Edeline Harris of Ann Arbor, who may be the only Haitian-born professional chef in the area.

Spain controlled Cuba and Puerto Rico; Great Britain ruled Bermuda, Jamaica and the Virgin Islands, among others, and France dominated several other countries, including Haiti.

"Haiti's food is very French-influenced, but with Caribbean flavors mixed in," Harris said in a telephone interview.

"You see it in the use of sauces, the way the sauces are made and the balancing of ingredients, where you have a perfect balance of flavors instead of tasting one dominant ingredient, like thyme or garlic."

And so it was with the food that Alcé prepared with the help of her daughter, Shirley Alcé, and family friend Gilbert Targette. Her menu ranged from everyday favorites made with signature Haitian flavors and staples to special-occasion dishes featuring luxury ingredients.

Each plate and pan offered a lesson. And so did the other guests, all natives of Haiti. Alcé's husband, Dr. Jean Alcé, a psychiatrist and faculty member at Wayne State University and a founder of Espoir, a Caribbean arts and culture group; Roland Wiener, an engineer, amateur historian, art collector and board member of the International Institute of Metropolitan Detroit; and Guerin C. Montilus, a Wayne State professor of anthropology.

Gathered around the table laden with so many tempting platters of food, everyone could tell there would be leftovers aplenty.

It made Alcé think of her grandmother. "After a meal such as this, she would say that you should wash your teeth and hang them,' she said, because you wouldn't need to eat again for a very long time."

And then the serving bowls began circulating.

The Meats

Meat and fish were featured in a half-dozen dishes, including the spicy pastries served before dinner and a second appetizer, made with smoked herring.

Smoked or salted fish is a mainstay in Haiti, where refrigeration is unavailable to many people. The fish can be shredded and cooked with rice or corn meal, or used in hundreds of other ways in any meal, including breakfast.

Fresh fish is always preferred, and Alcé prepared hers in a classic style: cleaned, scaled, marinated and fried whole, attractively garnished at serving time with rings of red onion and green pepper. She prefers red snapper, but king fish, doctor fish and goat fish are also popular in Haiti, she said.

Conch—the mollusk in the spiral shells that children look for at the beach—is as highly prized in Haiti as it is everywhere else. This night, Alcé cooked the snowy white, special-occasion meat in a flavorful, spicy Creole sauce.

Goat and chicken are probably the most frequently used meats in Haiti. Pork is much more expensive there and beef is rarely eaten—all for reasons that make sense in a small country with limited resources.

As Montilus, the anthropologist, pointed out, chickens can fend for themselves, and goats live on grass and leaves. They don't compete with humans for food as pigs do; they produce milk, are easy to handle and pen and require little space. Haiti's only beef cattle are owned by nomadic people, he said, so beef is available only when the herders pass through an area, perhaps as seldom as once a year.

Goat meat can be tough and have a strong flavor—but not prepared Alcé's way. Seasoned, boiled and then braised with tomato paste, lime juice and more seasonings, it was spicy and tender with a flavor like lamb.

Fruits, Veggies, Starches

Starches, fruits and vegetables are a larger part of the diet than meat and fish, however, and Alcé's table showcased their flavors and variations as well.

There was *banane pese*—pressed plantain, which is Haiti's version of fried plantain. After slices of green plantain are partially fried, they're removed from the skillet and flattened with a spatula. Then the pieces are dipped in saltwater for seasoning and fried again to finish cooking and take on a darker, crisper exterior. They have a neutral, subtle flavor that's a nice complement to spicy dishes, and they're eaten like a slice of bread, with the fingers.

The Haitian cookbook *Mountain Maid Best Made* says that *banane pese* is a traditional accompaniment to *griots,* the very spicy and quite delicious braised cubes of pork that Alcé also served.

Alcé offered two rice dishes: everyday *riz et pois,* of course, and *riz djon-djon,* made with a kind of dried black mushroom said to grow only in Haiti.

The expensive, prized fungi are generally unavailable in the United States, but Alcé found and purchased some in Miami. They infuse rice with a deeply earthy flavor and turn it an inky black; the more mushrooms, the deeper the color and the taste.

Alcé's husband and friends teased her, saying that the rice that night was the darkest they'd ever eaten—and that she should invite food writers to dinner more often.

But no dish is more beloved than simple *riz et pois.*

"I could not survive a day without rice and beans," Targette declared. Every Caribbean country has its own version of rice and peas—or peas and rice. Some countries make it with black beans, some use garbanzo beans, still others incorporate green peas or pigeon peas. But in Haiti, *riz et pois* must be made with small, red kidney beans in a multi-step process: First, the beans are simmered until they're almost done. Then they're removed from the cooking liquid and sautéed in oil with seasoning. Finally, they're returned to the liquid, rice is added and the two are cooked together.

"The rice drinks the beans' water," says Alcé, explaining why the dish turns out light and fluffy instead of soupy.

The *mais moulu*—cooked ground corn, or polenta—was a revelation. The Haitian version contained not only red beans and spices but coconut milk, which added richness, sweetness and a wonderfully exotic dimension to the dish.

Coconut milk or milk appear in both savory and sweet Haitian foods, such as the rich, coconut-flavored baked cassava pudding Alcé served for dessert.

And last, adding a burst of color and coolness to the table, was *salade Russe* or Russian salad, which is Haitian despite its name. With vegetables including red beets, yellow corn and orange carrots, it looks like a Caribbean sunset.

A Rare Treat

Harris, the Ann Arbor chef, does not specialize in Haitian cuisine at her restaurant, the Back-Alley Gourmet, but has begun to cook it occasionally.

"I'm slowly introducing it," she says. "I find that when I cook Haitian, everybody loves it. . . . It has so much flavor and such well balanced flavor."

When she gets in a Haitian cooking mood, she has a list of business and government contacts she calls and they come dashing over for a taste.

Like Alcé, she says Americans would enjoy Haitian food if they could taste it, but few get the chance. The Haitian government doesn't promote tourism, and few Americans visit the country.

Detroit briefly had a Haitian restaurant a few years ago, but it closed; most of the other local Caribbean restaurants are Jamaican.

They're fine, but they're not Haitian, Alcé says.

"We don't eat ackee and salt fish, as Jamaicans do," she says. And while every Jamaican restaurant serves curried goat, "There is no curry in Haiti." "We have a lot in common," she says, "but we are different."

Salade Russe

Salad:

   1 can (15 oz.) corn
   1 pound cooked green peas
   1 pound cooked green beans, or 1 can French-style cut
   1 pound carrots, peeled, cooked, diced
   1 pound cooked beets, diced

Vinaigrette:

   ¼ cup chopped onions
   ¼ cup chopped parsley
   Ground pepper to taste
   ⅓ cup white vinegar
   ½ cup olive oil
   Salt to taste

In a large bowl, combine all the salad ingredients. In a small bowl, whisk together the vinaigrette ingredients. Pour the vinaigrette over the salad ingredients. Refrigerate 2 hours to allow the flavors to meld before serving. Makes 12 side-dish servings.

(159 calories [41% from fat], 7 grams fat [1 gram sat. fat], 21 grams carbohydrate, 4 grams protein, 137 mg sodium, 0 mg cholesterol, 48 mg calcium, 6 grams fiber)

Banane Pese (Twice-Fried Plantain Slices)

Traditionally, Banane Pese is served as an accompaniment for Griots.

   ½ cup vegetable oil
   2 medium-size green plantains, peeled, cut crosswise into ½-inch slices
   2 cups salted water

In a large, heavy skillet, heat the oil over medium until a light haze forms above it. Add as many plantain slices as you can without crowding the pan, and brown about 2 minutes on each side. As they brown, transfer them to paper towels to drain. On a cutting board, use a spatula to press each slice into a flat round about ¼-inch thick and 2 inches in diameter. Dip the rounds in salted water and shake off the excess. Heat the oil and fry the rounds again, about 1 minute on each side. Drain on paper towels and serve at once. Makes 4 servings.

Adapted from *Mountain Maid Best Made Cookbook* (Mountain Maid Self-Help Project, $10). (202 calories [48% from fat], 11 grams fat [1 gram sat. fat], 29 grams carbohydrate, 1 gram protein, 4 mg sodium, 0 mg cholesterol, 3 mg calcium, 2 grams fiber)

Griots (Glazed and Braised Pork)

¼ cup vegetable oil

2 lbs. boneless pork loin, cut into 2-inch cubes

1 cup finely chopped onions

¼ cup finely chopped shallots, or substitute green onions
   (white part only)

1 cup strained fresh orange juice

¼ cup strained fresh lime juice

¼ cup water

¼ tsp. crumbled dried thyme

¼ tsp. salt

¼ tsp. freshly ground black pepper

¼ small hot pepper, minced

In a large, heavy skillet, heat the vegetable oil over medium until a light haze forms above it. Add the pork cubes. Turn frequently with a spoon and adjust the heat as necessary so the cubes brown richly and evenly without burning. Stir in the onions, shallots, orange juice, lime juice, water, thyme, salt, pepper and hot pepper. Bring to a boil over high heat, then cover the skillet, lower the heat and simmer 30 minutes. Uncover the skillet, increase the heat to high and, stirring frequently to prevent the meat from sticking, cook briskly 10 minutes or until the sauce thickens to a syrupy glaze. Makes 4 servings.

From Mountain *Maid Best Made Cookbook* (Mountain Maid Self-Help Project, $10). (414 calories [52% from fat], 24 grams fat [5 grams sat. fat], 13 grams carbohydrate, 36 grams protein, 367 mg sodium, 100 mg cholesterol, 46 mg calcium, 1 gram fiber)

Riz et Pois (Rice and Beans)

1 cup dried red kidney beans
1½ tsp. salt, divided
Freshly ground black pepper to taste
6 to 8 cups water
2 Tbsp. vegetable oil
2 to 3 cloves garlic, peeled, minced
1 green pepper, cored, chopped
2 green onions, chopped
1 to 2 Tbsp. fresh chopped parsley
½ tsp. black pepper
Salt to taste
½ tsp. ground cloves
1 Tbsp. butter
2 cups uncooked long-grain white rice

In a large sieve or colander, wash the beans under running water until the draining water runs clear. Transfer them to a heavy 3- or 4-quart saucepan. Add ½ teaspoon of the salt and the ground black pepper. Pour in 6 cups of the water. Bring to a boil over high heat. Reduce the heat to low and simmer, partially covered, 1½ hours or until the beans are tender but intact. Drain the beans and reserve the cooking liquid. In a large, heavy skillet, heat the vegetable oil. Add the garlic, green pepper, green onion, parsley, pepper, salt and cloves. Saute about 5 minutes. Add the beans and stir until heated through. Watch carefully for any sign of burning. Set aside. Measure out the bean cooking liquid and add enough water to make 4 cups. In a large sauce-pan, melt the butter over medium heat. When it is very hot, but not smoking, add the rice and stir 1–2 minutes, or until the grains turn somewhat milky and opaque. Stir in the 4 cups of reserved liquid and water, the remaining 1 teaspoon of salt and more ground black pepper to taste. Bring to a hard boil. Reduce the heat, add the cooked bean mixture, cover tightly and reduce the heat to the lowest possible setting. Simmer 20 minutes, or until the rice is tender and has absorbed all the liquid. Taste for seasoning and adjust if necessary with salt and pepper. Fluff the rice and beans with a fork and serve hot. Makes 6 servings.

Adapted from *Mountain Maid Best Made Cookbook* (Mountain Maid Self-Help Project, $10). (395 calories [14% from fat], 6 grams fat [1 gram sat. fat], 72 grams carbohydrate, 12 grams protein, 654 mg sodium, 0 mg cholesterol, 76 mg calcium, 8 grams fiber)

Conch in Creole Sauce

1 lb. shelled conch, cleaned, skinned
2 limes, halved
¼ cup unsalted butter
1 medium onion, peeled, halved, sliced
3 cloves garlic, peeled, minced
1½ tsp. minced shallots
1 tomato, peeled, seeded, chopped
¾ cup water
3 Tbsp. tomato paste
1½ tsp. minced fresh thyme, or ½ tsp. dried thyme
½ Scotch bonnet chile, minced
Salt and black pepper to taste
Hot cooked rice

Pound the conch to ⅛-inch thick with a mallet; cut it into 1½-inch squares. Place the conch in a medium bowl; squeeze the limes over the top. Add the lime rinds and water to cover. Cover and refrigerate 1–1½ hours. Drain and discard the rinds. In a Dutch oven or large pot, melt the butter. Add the onion, garlic and shallots and saute until soft but not brown, about 5 minutes. Stir in the tomato, water, tomato paste, thyme, minced chile and conch. Heat over medium to boiling; reduce the heat to low. Simmer, partially covered, until the conch is fork tender, 45–50 minutes, stirring occasionally. Season to taste with salt and pepper. Serve over hot cooked rice. Makes 4 servings.

Adapted from *Mountain Maid Best Made Cookbook* (Mountain Maid Self-Help Project, $10). (341 calories [38% from fat], 14 grams fat [7 grams sat. fat], 16 grams carbohydrate, 36 grams protein, 167 mg sodium, 122 mg cholesterol, 147 mg calcium, 2 grams fiber)

Notes

1. Karen Dimanche Davis, personal communication, January 11, 2009.

2. Despite the fact that Haitians do not have a single term to refer to all religious rituals associated with African ancestral spirits, I use the term *Vodou* to refer to all Africanist spiritual practices in general. See Michael Largey, *Vodou Nation: Haitian Art Music and Cultural Nationalism* (Chicago: University of Chicago Press, 2006), 243, n. 2, for a detailed explanation of the history of the term *Vodou* in Haitian scholarship.

3. For more information on the economy of Haiti in the nineteenth century, see Michel-Rolph Trouillot, *Haiti—State against Nation: The Origins and Legacy of Duvalierism* (New York: Monthly Review Press, 1990).

4. Jean Price-Mars, *So Spoke the Uncle,* trans. Magdaline W. Shannon (Washington, D.C.: Three Continents Press, 1983).

5. J. Michael Dash, *Literature and Ideology in Haiti, 1915-1961* (Totowa, N.J.: Barnes and Noble, 1981), 78.

6. Largey, *Vodou Nation,* 203. Also see Kate Ramsey, "Without One Ritual Note: Folklore Performance and the Haitian State, 1935-1946," *Radical History Review* 84 (2002): 7-42.

7. Lois Wilcken, "Power, Ambivalence, and the Remaking of Haitian Vodoun Music in New York," *Latin American Music Review* 13, no. 1 (Spring-Summer 1992): 8.

8. Oscar G. Sonneck, *Early Concert Life in America* (New York: Musurgia, 1949), 27.

9. Ibid., 29.

10. John Smith Kendall, *History of New Orleans* (Chicago: Lewis, 1922), 1: 85.

11. Jean Fouchard, *Plaisirs de Saint-Domingue* (Port-au-Prince: Editions Henri Deschamps, 1955).

12. René J. Le Gardeur, Jr., *The First New Orleans Theatre, 1792–1803* (New Orleans: Leeward Books, 1963).

13. John G. Cale, "French Secular Music in Saint-Domingue (1750–1795) Viewed as a Factor in America's Musical Growth" (Ph.D. dissertation, Louisiana State University and Agricultural and Mechanical College, 1971).

14. *Statistical Yearbook*, U.S. Department of Justice, Immigration and Naturalization Service (Washington, D.C.: Government Printing Office, 2000), table 2, 8–9.

15. Gage Averill, *A Day for the Hunter, A Day for the Prey: Music and Power in Haiti* (Chicago: University of Chicago Press, 1997), 113.

16. Ibid., 114.

17. Nina Glick-Schiller and Georges Fouron, *Georges Woke Up Laughing: Long-Distance Nationalism and the Search for Home* (Durham, N.C.: Duke University Press, 2001), 12.

18. Haitians refer to AIDS by its French acronym, SIDA.

19. Paul Farmer, *AIDS and Accusation: Haiti and the Geography of Blame* (Berkeley: University of California Press, 1991), 2–4.

20. Ibid., 2. Also see Peter Moses and John Moses, "Haiti and the Acquired Immune Deficiency Syndrome," *Annals of Internal Medicine* 99, no. 4 (1983): 565.

21. Robert Lawless, *Haiti's Bad Press* (Rochester, Vt.: Schenkman, 1992), 17.

22. Alex Stepick, *Pride against Prejudice: Haitians in the United States* (Needham Heights, Mass.: Allyn and Bacon, 1998), 9.

23. Flore Zéphir, *The Haitian Americans* (Westport, Conn.: Greenwood Press, 2004), 94.

24. Michael Largey, "How to Watch a Voodoo Movie: Rules for a Postmodern Age," *The Ryder* (October 1998), 29.

25. Melville J. Herskovits, *Life in a Haitian Valley* (New York: Alfred A. Knopf, 1937), 139.

26. For detailed accounts of Haitian Vodou ceremonies, see Karen McCarthy Brown, *Mama Lola: A Haitian Priestess in Brooklyn* (Berkeley: University of California Press, 2001).

27. Wilcken, "Power, Ambivalence," 15–25.

28. For more detailed information about the group's personnel and repertoire, see

http://www.makandal.org, accessed December 20, 2008.

29. For more information on Augustin's National Heritage Award, see http://www. nea.gov/honors/heritage/fellows/NHFIntro.php?year=1999, accessed December 20, 2008.

30. See http://www.haitiprogres.com, accessed December 20, 2008.

31. See http://www.haitiantimes.com, accessed December 20, 2008.

32. See http://www.haiti-observateur.com, accessed December 20, 2008.

33. See http://www.haitienmarche.com, accessed December 20, 2008.

34. See http://www.bostonhaitian.com, accessed December 20, 2008.

35. Michel S. Laguerre, *Diasporic Citizenship: Haitian Americans in Transnational America* (New York: St. Martin's Press, 1998), 130.

36. Ibid., 130.

37. Radio Tropicale (http://www.radiotropicale.com); Radio Soleil d'Haiti (http://www.radiosoleil.com); Radio Pa Nou (http://www.radiopanou.com). Radio Tropicale and Radio Soleil offer free access from the Internet; Radio Lakay's Web site is still under construction; and Radio Pa Nou charges a membership fee.

38. "Our Radio," as people from northern Haiti say; http://www.radiokeenam.com. For more information on radio stations, see http://www.mezanmi.com/radio. aspx?cstep=viewall.

39. Laguerre, *Diasporic Citizenship*, 134.

40. For a list of Haitian radio stations, see http://www.anselme.homestead.com/ RADIO.html.

41. See http://www.radiolumiere.org, accessed December 20, 2008.

42. Stepick, *Pride against Prejudice*, 60.

43. Maria Patricia Fernández-Kelly and Richards Schauffler, "Divided Fates: Immigrant Children in a Restructured U.S. Economy," *International Migration Review* 38, no. 4 (Winter 1994): 662–689; quoted in Stepick, *Pride against Prejudice*, 71.

44. See http://www.haitianstudies.umb.edu, accessed December 20, 2008.

45. See http://ccde.umb.edu/summerinstitute/haitiancreole, accessed December 20, 2008.

46. Marita-Constance Supan, IHM, "Dangerous Memory: Mother M. Theresa Maxis Duchemin and the Michigan Congregation of Sisters, I.H.M.," in *Building Sisterhood: A Feminist History of the Sisters, Servants of the Immaculate Heart of Mary* (Syracuse, N.Y.: Syracuse University Press, 1997), 34.

47. Ibid., 35.

48. Ibid., 35; Grace H. Sherwood, "The Oblate Sisters of Providence: America's First Negro Religious Order," part 1, *The Voice of the Students and Alumni of St Mary's* 7, no. 3 (1931): 14–15.

49. Supan, "Dangerous Memory," 35.

50. Ibid., 36.

51. Sister M. Rosalita, *No Greater Service: The History of the Congregation of the Sisters, Servants of the Immaculate Heart of Mary, Monroe, Michigan, 1845–1945* (Monroe, Mich.: Congregation of the Sisters, Servants of the Immaculate Heart of Mary), 42.

52. Ibid., 43.

53. Ibid., 44.

54. Supan, "Dangerous Memory," 40.

55. Ibid.

56. Ibid., 42.

57. Ibid., 43.

58. Ibid., 47.

59. Ibid., 50.

60. Ibid., 52.

61. Ibid.

62. Margaret Gannon, ed., *Paths of Daring, Deeds of Hope*. Scranton, Penn.: Immaculate Heart of Mary Sisters, 1992), 4.

63. See http://www.marygrove.edu, accessed December 20, 2008.

64. Chantalle Francesca Verna, "Beyond the Immigration Centers: A History of Haitian Community in Three Michigan Cities, 1966–1998" (M.A. thesis, Michigan State University, 2000), 35.

65. Ibid., 41–42.

66. Jean Alcé, interview, Detroit, July 6, 2007.

67. See http://www.haiti-sa.org/modern/detroit/detroit_location_of_the_community.php, accessed July 2, 2008; Karen Davis, personal communication, January 11, 2009.

68. *"Ti Koze Sou Ayiti* ('A Little News about Haiti')," *Sacred Heart Church Program* 3, no. 4 (2008): 1–8.

69. Adeline Auguste, interview, Detroit, July 8, 2007.

70. See http://www.peckham.org, accessed December 20, 2008.

71. See http://www.bethany.org, accessed December 20, 2008; Verna, "Beyond the Immigration Centers," 67.

72. Confidential interview, Grand Rapids, Mich.

73. See http://www.grcc.cc.mi.us, accessed December 20, 2008.

74. See http://www.kc-tc.org, accessed December 20, 2008.

75. Dieuseul Benoit, interview, Grand Rapids, Mich., September 28, 2007; my translation.

76. Jean-Claude Dutès, "Cultural Relocation and Adjustment," *Graduate Post* (Michigan State University) 4, no. 2 (Spring 1997): 19–22.

77. Jean-Claude Dutès, interview, East Lansing, Mich., September 27, 2007.

78. See Karen Richman, *Migration and Vodou* (Gainesville, Fla.: University Press of Florida, 2005), for a compelling account of how illiterate Haitian immigrants use cassettes to establish connections with family members in the United States.

79. Glick-Schiller and Fouron, *Georges Woke Up Laughing*.

80. Karen Dimanche Davis, personal communication, April 15, 2009.

81. Verna, "Beyond the Immigration Centers," 87.

82. Marie-José Alcé, interview, Oak Park, Mich., July 17, 2007.

83. Adeline Auguste, interview, Detroit, July 8, 2007.

84. Marie-José Alcé, interview.

85. Danielle Desroches, interview.

86. Ibid.

87. Guérin Montilus, personal communication, Detroit, September 18, 2007.

88. See Maurice Halbwachs, *On Collective Memory*, ed. and trans. by Lewis A. Coser (Chicago: University of Chicago Press, 1992).

89. Largey, *Vodou Nation*, 10.

90. Bambi B. Schieffelin and Rachelle Charlier Doucet, "The 'Real' Haitian Creole: Ideology, Metalinguistics, and Orthographic Choice." In *Language Ideologies: Practice and Theory* (New York: Oxford University Press, 1998), 297.

91. For a vividly described situation in which an English-speaking Haitian child helps her Kreyòl-speaking mother in a meeting with a lawyer, see Brown, *Mama Lola*, 109–133.

92. Mathieu Pierre, interview, Comstock Park, Mich., October 5, 2007.

93. Marie Soledad Nelson, interview, Southfield, Mich., July 6, 2007.

94. Ibid.

95. Susan Kalčik, "Ethnic Foodways in America: Symbol and the Performance of Identity," in *Ethnic and Regional Foodways in the United States: The Performance of Group Identity*, ed. by Linda Keller Brown and Kay Mussell (Knoxville: University of Tennessee Press, 1985), 40.

96. Desroches, interview.

97. For more information on Haitian Flag Day, see http://www.haitiantreasures.
com/HT_haitian_flag.day1.htm.

98. Catherine Auguste, interview, Detroit, July 21, 2007.

99. Marie-José Alcé, interview.

100. Margareth Corkery, interview, Northville, Mich., July 8, 2008.

101. Marie-José Alcé, interview.

102. Penny Godboldo, interview, Detroit, October 23, 2007.

103. Ibid.

104. Ibid.

105. Ramsey, "Without One Ritual Note."

106. "Contributions from the Caribbean, Part 3: A Gift for Everyone," *Krik Krak* 7, no.
2 (May 2001): 9.

107. See http://www.centralfreemethodist.org, accessed December 20, 2008.

108. Confidential interview.

109. Jean Alcé, personal communication, January 10, 2009.

110. Wilcken, "Power, Ambivalence."

111. For more on the music of the denominations of Vodou religion, see Michael
Largey, "Haiti and the French Caribbean," in *Caribbean Currents: Caribbean
Music from Rumba to Reggae,* rev. ed., ed. by Peter Manuel, Kenneth Bilby, and
Michael Largey (Philadelphia: Temple University Press, 2006), 146–151.

112. Philip Singer, *The Haitians, the Healers, and the Anthropologist: Two Case Studies.* Traditional Healing Productions, Southfield, Mich., 1997.

113. Verna, "Beyond the Immigration Centers," 105.

114. Ibid., 107.

115. Ibid., 107–108.

116. "Vision Statement: Caribbean American Cultural Center," *Krik Krak* 1, no. 1
(Summer 1993): 3.

117. "Espoir: A Decade of Hope," copy in personal collection.

118. "Espoir and Eye Care to Sponsor Haitian Art Sale," *Krik Krak* 1, no. 2 (Fall 1993): 1.

119. Edwidge Dandicat's book of short stories, *Krik? Krak!* (New York: Soho Press,
1995), also borrows from this tradition. See Guérin Montilus, "Krik Krak! What's
in a Name?" *Krik Krak* 1, no. 1 (Summer 1993): 1–2, for a literary interpretation of
the meaning of storytelling in Haiti.

120. "History of Espoir," *Krik Krak* 1, no. 1 (Summer 1993): 4.

121. Melissa Worden, "Students Make a Difference Assisting Haitian Refugees," *Krik*

Krak 1, no. 3 (Winter 1994): 1.

122. Espoir program for "Le Neuviéme Banquet Annuel de Charité, 'It Takes a Whole Village to Raise a Child,'" Westin Hotel, Detroit, November 19, 1994.

123. "MAAH 1997 Winter Exhibit Schedule," *Krik Krak* 4, no. 1 (Winter 1997): 1.

124. Adeline Auguste, personal communication, October 21, 2008.

125. See http://www.umd.umich.edu/univ/ur/press_releases/dec03/haitian_ pr.html, accessed November 12, 2008.

126. "Tribute Series Honors the Life and Legacy of C. L. R. James," *Krik Krak* 7, no. 1 (January 2001): 1.

127. "Black History Month: A Tribute to the Fight for Social Revolution," copy in personal collection.

128. Raymond Laurin, "'Prelude to the Celebration of the Bicentennial of the Independence of Haiti' Planned for May in Detroit," *Krik Krak* 8, no. 1 (March 2002): 1-2.

129. "Cuban Coalition Meeting Draws Crowd," *Krik Krak* 6, no. 2 (May 2000): 4.

130. "Immigration Double Standard in the News," *Krik Krak* 6, no. 3 (September 2000): 8.

131. Sonja Gildon, "Annual Essay Scholarship Promotes Understanding!" *Krik Krak* 1, no. 1 (Summer 1993): 2.

132. See http://www.hngd.com/biography.htm, accessed December 20, 2008.

133. Nelson, interview.

134. "1804—Celebrating a Legacy—2004," Haitian Network Group of Detroit program, copy in personal collection.

135. "Eyes on Haiti: The Reel Deal, 2006," Haitian Network Group of Detroit program, copy in personal collection.

136. Ibid.

137. Corkery, interview.

138. Julie Fleming, "The Pichon Project," *Zanmi Detroit* 3, no. 1 (October 2004): 1.

139. See http://www.myccco.com, accessed December 15, 2008.

140. "Carival: 9th Annual Caribbean International Festival, 2001," copy in personal collection.

141. See http://www.haitioutreachmission.org, accessed December 17, 2008.

142. Dominique Mondé-Matthews, interview, Southfield, Mich., October 22, 2007.

143. Ibid.

144. Desroches, interview.

For Further Reference

Arthur, Charles. *Haiti in Focus: A Guide to the People, Politics and Culture.* New York: Interlink Books, 2002.

Averill, Gage. *A Day for the Hunter, A Day for the Prey: Music and Power in Haiti.* Chicago: University of Chicago Press, 1997.

Bellegarde-Smith, Patrick. *Haiti: The Breached Citadel.* Boulder, Colo.: Westview Press, 1990.

"Black History Month: 'A Tribute to the Fight for Social Revolution.' The 100 Year Anniversary Celebration of the Birth of C. L. R. James, 1901–2001." Announcement flyer in personal collection.

Brown, Karen McCarthy. "Alourdes: A Case Study of Moral Leadership in Haitian Vodou." In *Saints and Virtues,* ed. by John Stratton Hawley, 144–167. Berkeley: University of California Press, 1987.

———. *Mama Lola: A Vodou Priestess in Brooklyn.* Berkeley: University of California Press, 2001.

———. "Systematic Remembering, Systematic Forgetting: Ogou in Haiti." In *Africa's Ogun: Old World and New,* ed. by Sandra T. Barnes, 65–89. Bloomington: Indiana University Press, 1989.

Cale, John G. "French Secular Music in Saint-Domingue (1750–1795) Viewed as a Factor in America's Musical Growth." Ph.D. dissertation, Louisiana State University and Agricultural and Mechanical College, 1971.

"Carival: 9th Annual Caribbean International Festival." Program for Carival 2001 in personal collection.

Catanese, Anthony V. *Haitians: Migration and Diaspora*. Boulder, Colo.: Westview Press, 1999.

Chierici, Rose-Marie Cassagnol. *Demele: "Making It"—Migration and Adaptation Among Haitian Boat People in the United States*. New York: AMS Press, 1991.

CIA World Factbook. Https://www.cia.gov/library/publications/the-world-factbook/geos/ha.html, accessed December 20, 2008.

City of Boston, Mayor's Office of New Bostonians. *Imagine All the People: Haitian Immigrants in Boston*. March 2007. Http://www.cityofboston.gov/bra/pdf/ResearchPublications//IAP%20Haitian%20Profile.pdf, accessed May 27, 2008.

"Contributions from the Caribbean, Part 3: A Gift for Everyone." *Krik Krak* 7, no. 2 (May 2001): 3, 9.

Cosentino, Donald J., ed. *Sacred Arts of Haitian Vodou*. Los Angeles: UCLA Fowler Museum of Cultural History, 1995.

Courlander, Harold. *The Drum and the Hoe: The Life and Lore of the Haitian People*. 1960; Berkeley: University of California Press, 1986.

———. *Haiti Singing*. New York: Cooper Square, 1939.

"Cuban Coalition Meeting Draws Crowd." *Krik Krak* 6, no. 2 (May 2000): 4.

Dandicat, Edwidge. *Krik? Krak!* New York: Soho Press, 1995.

Dash, J. Michael. *Culture and Customs of Haiti*. Westport, Conn.: Greenwood Press, 2001.

———. *Haiti and the United States: National Stereotypes and the Literary Imagination*. New York: St. Martin's Press, 1988.

———. *Literature and Ideology in Haiti, 1915–1961*. Totowa, N.J.: Barnes and Noble, 1981.

Desmangles, Leslie. *The Faces of the Gods: Vodou and Roman Catholicism in Haiti*. Chapel Hill: University of North Carolina Press, 1992.

Dumervé, Etienne Constintin Eugène Moïse. *Histoire de la musique en Haïti*. Port-au-Prince: Imprimerie des Antilles, 1968.

Dunham, Katherine. *Island Possessed*. Chicago: University of Chicago Press, 1994.

Dutès, Jean-Claude. "Cultural Relocation and Adjustment." *Graduate Post* (Michigan State University) 4, no. 2 (Spring 1997): 19–22.

"1804—Celebrating a Legacy—2004." Program for the Haitian Network Group of Detroit, 2004. Program in personal collection.

"Espoir and Eye Care to Sponsor Haitian Art Sale," *Krik Krak* 1, no. 2 (Fall 1993): 1.

Farmer, Paul. *AIDS and Accusation: Haiti and the Geography of Blame.* Berkeley: University of California Press, 1991.

——. *The Uses of Haiti.* Monroe, Maine: Common Courage Press, 1994.

Fernández-Kelly, Maria Patricia, and Richard Schauffler. "Divided Fates: Immigrant Children in a Restructured U.S. Economy." *International Migration Review* 38, no. 4 (Winter 1994): 662–689.

Fleming, Julie. "The Pichon Project." *Zanmi Detroit* 3, no. 1 (October 2004): 1.

Fouchard, Jean. *Plaisirs de Saint-Domingue.* Port-au-Prince: Editions Henri Deschamps, 1988.

Freeman, Bryant C. ed., *Haitian-English Dictionary,* 5th ed. Lawrence: Institute of Haitian Studies, University of Kansas, 2004.

Gannon, Margaret. *Mother Theresa Maxis Duchemin.* Scranton, Penn.: Immaculate Heart of Mary Sisters, 1978.

——, ed. *Paths of Daring, Deeds of Hope.* Scranton, Penn.: Immaculate Heart of Mary Sisters, 1992.

Gildon, Sonja. "Annual Essay Scholarship Promotes Understanding!" *Krik Krak* 1, no. 1 (Summer 1993): 2.

Glazier, Jack. *Ethnicity in Michigan: People and Issues.* East Lansing: Michigan State University Press, 2001.

Glick-Schiller, Nina, and Georges Fouron. *Georges Woke Up Laughing: Long-Distance Nationalism and the Search for Home.* Durham, N.C.: Duke University Press, 2001.

Glick-Schiller, Nina, Josh Dewind, Marie Lucie Brutus, Carolle Charles, Georges Fouron, and Antoine Thomas. "All in the Same Boat? Unity and Diversity in Haitian Organizing in New York," In *Caribbean Life in New York City: Sociocultural Dimesions,* ed. by Constance R. Sutton and Elsa M. Chaney, 182–201. New York: Center for Migration Studies of New York, 1987.

Halbwachs, Maurice. *On Collective Memory,* ed. and trans. by Lewis A. Coser. Chicago: University of Chicago Press, 1992.

Hayes, Helene. *U.S. Immigration Policy and the Undocumented: Ambivalent Laws, Furtive Lives.* Westport, Conn.: Praeger, 2001.

Herskovits, Melville J. *Life in a Haitian Valley.* New York: Alfred A. Knopf, 1937.

"History of Espoir," *Krik Krak* 1, no. 1 (Summer 1993): 4.

Holly, James Theodore. "A Vindication of the Capacity of the Negro Race for Self-Government, and Civilized Progress, as Demonstrated by Historical Events of the Haytian Revolution; and the Subsequent Acts of that People since Their

National Independence." In *Black Separatism and the Caribbean 1860,* ed, by Howard H. Bell, 17-66. Ann Arbor: University of Michigan Press, 1970.

Hurbon, Laënnec. "American Fantasy and Haitian Vodou." In *Sacred Arts of Haitian Vodou,* ed. by Donald Cosentino, 181-197. Los Angeles: UCLA Fowler Museum of Cultural History, 1995.

"Immigration Double Standard in the News." *Krik Krak* 6, no. 3 (September 2000): 8.

James, C. L. R. *The Black Jacobins: Toussaint L'Ouverture and the San Domingo Revolution.* New York: Vintage, 1963.

Kalčik, Susan. "Ethnic Foodways in America: Symbol and the Performance of Identity." In *Ethnic and Regional Foodways in the United States: The Performance of Group Identity,* ed. by Linda Keller Brown and Kay Mussell, 37-65. Knoxville: University of Tennessee Press, 1985.

Kay, Jennifer. "Restavek Problem Exposed in Florida." *Boston Haitian Reporter* 6, no. 11 (November 2007): 10.

Kendall, John Smith. *History of New Orleans,* 3 vols. Chicago: Lewis, 1922.

Laguerre, Michel S. *Diasporic Citizenship: Haitian Americans in Transnational America.* New York: St. Martin's Press, 1998.

Largey, Michael. "Composing a Haitian Cultural Identity: Haitian Elites, African Ancestry, and Musical Composition." *Black Music Research Journal* 14, no. 2 (1994): 99-117.

———. "Haiti and the French Caribbean." In *Caribbean Currents: Caribbean Music from Rumba to Reggae,* rev. ed., ed. by Peter Manuel, Kenneth Bilby, and Michael Largey, 141-176. Philadelphia: Temple University Press, 2006.

———. "How to Watch a Voodoo Movie: Rules for a Postmodern Age." *The Ryder* (October 1998): 28-31.

———. "Politics on the Pavement: Haitian Rara as a Traditionalizing Process." *Journal of American Folklore* 113, no. 449 (Summer 2000): 239-254.

———. *Vodou Nation: Haitian Art Music and Cultural Nationalism.* Chicago: University of Chicago Press, 2006.

Laurin, Raymond. "'Prelude to the Celebration of the Bicentennial of the Independence of Haiti' Planned for May in Detroit." *Krik Krak* 8, no. 1 (March 2002): 1-2.

Lawless, Robert. *Haiti's Bad Press.* Rochester, Vt.: Schenkman, 1992.

Le Gardeur, René J. Jr. *The First New Orleans Theatre, 1792-1803.* New Orleans: Leeward Books, 1963.

Lemay, Michael, and Elliott Robert Barkan. *US Immigration and Naturalization Laws and Issues: A Documented History.* Westport, Conn.: Greenwood Press, 1999.

"MAAH 1997 Exhibit Schedule." *Krik Krak* 4, no. 1 (Winter 1997): 1.

Miller, Jake C. *The Plight of the Haitian Refugees.* New York: Praeger, 1984.

Montilus, Guérin C. "Krik Krak! What's in a Name!" *Krik Krak* 1, no. 1 (Summer 1993): 1-2.

Moreau de Saint-Méry, Médéric Louis-Elie. *Description topographique, physique, civile, politique et historique de la partie française de l'isle Saint-Domingue.* Philadelphia: by the author, 1797-98.

Moses, Peter, and John Moses. "Haiti and the Acquired Immune Deficiency Syndrome." *Annals of Internal Medicine* 99, no. 4 (1983): 565.

New York City Department of City Planning. *The Newest New Yorkers: An Analysis of Immigration into NYC during the 1980s.* New York: Department of City Planning, 1992.

Nicholls, David. *From Dessalines to Duvalier: Race, Colour, and National Independence in Haiti.* Cambridge, U.K.: Cambridge University Press, 1979.

———. *Haiti in Caribbean Context: Ethnicity, Economy and Revolt.* New York: St. Martin's Press, 1985.

Pamphile, Léon D. *Haitians and African Americans: A Heritage of Tragedy and Hope.* Gainesville: University Press of Florida, 2001.

Paquin, Lyonel. *The Haitians: Class and Color Politics.* New York: Multi-Type, 1983.

Plummer, Brenda Gayle. *Haiti and the Great Powers, 1902-1915.* Baton Rouge: Louisiana State University Press, 1988.

———. *Haiti and the United States: The Psychological Moment.* Athens: University of Georgia Press, 1992.

Price-Mars, Jean. *So Spoke the Uncle,* trans. Magdaline W. Shannon. Washington, D.C.: Three Continents Press, 1983.

Ramsey, Kate. "Without One Ritual Note: Folklore Performance and the Haitian State, 1935-1946." *Radical History Review* 84 (2002): 7-42.

Renda, Mary A. *Taking Haiti: Military Occupation and the Culture of U.S. Imperialism.* Chapel Hill: University of North Carolina Press, 2001.

"Rep. Dorcena Forry Honored for Legislative Work." *Boston Haitian Reporter* 7, no. 2 (February 2003): 4.

Richman, Karen E. *Migration and Vodou.* Gainesville: University Press of Florida, 2005.

Rosalita, Sister M., I.H.M. *The Motherhouse and Missions: Congregation of the Sisters, Servants of the Immaculate Heart of Mary, Monroe, Michigan, 1845-1945.* Monroe, Mich.: Congregation of the Sisters, Servants of the Immaculate Heart of

Mary, 1948.

———. *No Greater Service: The History of the Congregation of the Sisters, Servants of the Immaculate Heart of Mary, Monroe, Michigan, 1845–1945.* Monroe, Mich: Congregation of the Sisters, Servants of the Immaculate Heart of Mary, 1948.

Schieffelin, Bambi B., and Rachelle Charlier Doucet. "The 'Real' Haitian Creole: Ideology, Metalinguistics, and Orthographic Choice." In *Language Ideologies: Practice and Theory,* ed. by Bambi B. Schieffelin, Kathryn A. Woolard, Paul V. Kroskrity, 285–316. New York: Oxford University Press, 1998.

Schmidt, Hans. *The United States Occupation of Haiti, 1915–1934.* 1971; New Brunswick, N.J.: Rutgers University Press, 1995.

Shannon, Magdaline W. *Jean Price-Mars, the Haitian Elite and the American Occupation, 1915–1935.* New York: St. Martin's Press, 1996.

Sherwood, Grace H. "The Oblate Sisters of Providence: America's First Negro Religious Order," part 1. *The Voice of the Students and Alumni of St. Mary's* 7, no. 3 (1931): 14–15.

Singer, Philip. *The Haitians, the Healers, and the Anthropologist: Two Case Studies.* Film, 100 minutes, color. Traditional Healing Productions, Southfield, Mich., 1997.

Sonneck, Oscar G. *Early Concert Life in America.* New York: Musurgia, 1949.

Stafford, Susan Buchanan. "Language and Identity: Haitians in New York City." In *Caribbean Life in New York City: Sociocultural Dimesions,* ed. by Constance R. Sutton and Elsa M. Chaney, 202–218. New York: Center for Migration Studies of New York, 1987.

Statistical Yearbook. U.S. Department of Justice, Immigration and Naturalization Service. Washington, D.C.: Government Printing Office, 2000, table 2, 8–9.

Stepick, Alex. *Pride against Prejudice: Haitians in the United States.* Needham Heights, Mass.: Allyn and Bacon, 1998.

Supan, Marita-Constance, IHM. "Dangerous Memory: Mother M. Theresa Maxis Duchemin and the Michigan Congregation of Sisters, I.H.M." In *Building Sisterhood: A Feminist History of the Sisters, Servants of the Immaculate Heart of Mary,* 31–57. Syracuse, N.Y.: Syracuse University Press, 1997.

"*Ti Koze Sou Ayiti* ('A Little News about Haiti')." *Sacred Heart Church Program* 3, no. 4 (2008): 1–8.

"Tribute Series Honors the Life and Legacy of C. L. R. James." *Krik Krak* 7, no. 1 (January 2001): 1.

Trouillot, Michel-Rolph. *Haiti—State against Nation: The Origins and Legacy of Du-*

valierism. New York: Monthly Review Press, 1990.

————. *Silencing the Past: Power and the Production of History.* Boston: Beacon Press, 1995.

Valdman, Albert. "The Linguistic Situation of Haiti." In *Haiti—Today and Tomorrow: An Interdisciplinary Study,* ed. by Charles R. Foster and Albert Valdman, 77–100. Lanham, Md.: University Presses of America, 1984.

————, ed. *Haitian Creole-English Bilingual Dictionary.* Bloomington: Indiana University Creole Institute, n.d.

Verna, Chantalle Francesca. "Beyond the Immigration Centers: A History of Haitian Community in Three Michigan Cities, 1966–1998." M.A. thesis, Michigan State University, 2000.

"Vision Statement: Caribbean American Cultural Center," *Krik Krak* 1, no. 1 (Summer 1993): 3.

Wilcken, Lois E. 1992. "Power, Ambivalence, and the Remaking of Haitian Vodoun Music in New York." *Latin American Music Review* 13, no. 1 (1992): 1–32.

Worden, Melissa. "Students Make a Difference Assisting Haitian Refugees." *Krik Krak* 1, no. 3 (Winter 1994): 1, 3.

Zéphir, Flore. *The Haitian Americans.* Westport, Conn.: Greenwood Press, 2004.

Index